AIRPORT INTERIORS

AIRPORT INTERIORS
DESIGN FOR BUSINESS

Steve Thomas-Emberson

WILEY
1807
WILEY
2007

Front Cover: The Eyecon Bar, Copenhagen International Airport, Denmark
Frontispiece: Rejuve, Heathrow Airport Terminal 1
Right: Sydney Airport, Australia

Published in Great Britain in 2007 by John Wiley & Sons Ltd

Copyright © 2007   John Wiley & Sons Ltd, The Atrium, Southern Gate, Chichester, West Sussex PO19 8SQ, England Telephone (+44) 1243 779777

Email (for orders and customer service enquiries): cs-books@wiley.co.uk
Visit our Home Page on www.wiley.com

Anniversary Logo Design: Richard Pacifico

Other Wiley Editorial Offices

John Wiley & Sons Inc, 111 River Street, Hoboken, NJ 07030, USA

Jossey-Bass, 989 Market Street, San Francisco, CA 94103-1741, USA

Wiley-VCH Verlag GmbH, Boschstr 12, D-69469 Weinheim, Germany

John Wiley & Sons Australia Ltd, 42 McDougall Street, Milton, Queensland 4064, Australia

John Wiley & Sons (Asia) Pte Ltd, 2 Clementi Loop #02-01, Jin Xing Distripark, Singapore 129809

John Wiley & Sons Canada Ltd, 5353 Dundas Street West, Suite 400, Etobicoke, Ontario M9B 6H8, Canada

Wiley also publishes its books in a variety of electronic formats. Some content that appears in print may not be available in electronic books.

Executive Commissioning Editor: Helen Castle
Project Editor: Miriam Swift
Publishing Assistant: Calver Lezama

ISBN 978 0 470 03475 0

Cover design © Artmedia Press Ltd, UK
Page design and layouts by Artmedia Press Ltd, UK

Printed and bound by Conti Tipocolor, Italy

CONTENTS

For Lydia and Matthew

ACKNOWLEDGEMENTS

First, huge thanks must go to Helen Castle for her constant encouragement, her checks on progress and her support of the book from the presentation day in the beginning. Grateful support must be acknowledged from the very many creative geniuses within the design business who backed the idea and the resulting book from the start: people such as Robbie Gill of The Design Solution for his help in opening his door and others; Rodney Kinsman for providing humour and inspiration; Steve Collis of JHP for project guidance; and lastly Doug Barber of Barber Design, who asked: 'How can you have an airport interiors book without covering business lounges?' You cannot – I took your advice!

The book is a collection of case studies, so sincere thanks go to all the retailers, food and beverage providers and other members of the leisure industry for opening their souls to scrutiny.

Lastly, I could not possibly have managed without Joan Coster's continual secretarial support and promptness in her work, and James Cartwright for technical help in collating the images for the book – my thanks to you both.

PHOTO CREDITS

The author and the publisher gratefully acknowledge the people who gave their permission to reproduce material in this book. While every effort has been made to contact copyright holders for their permission to reprint material the publishers would be grateful to hear from any copyright holder who is not acknowledged here and will undertake to rectify any errors or omissions in future editions.

Front Cover Photos Arne V. Petersen © Copenhagen Airports A/S.
pp 2, 10, 100-103, 165-166, 176-185, 202-207 © The Design Solution; pp 4-5, 6 right, 13, 104-113 © Sydney Airport Corporation; pp 7 right, 216-223 © Shanghai Tang; pp 14, 16 © courtesy BAA Heathrow; pp 18 (b) © Hulton-Deutsch collection/Corbis; pp 19 © JP Laffont/Sygma/Corbis; pg 20 © KERIM OKTEN/epa/Corbis; pp 23-25 © Aéroports de Paris; pp 27-35 Photos Arne V. Petersen © Copenhagen Airports A/S; pp 36-43 © Aena /Agaena; pp 44-9 © Bristol International Airport; pp 50, 54-57 © JHP/ Photos Jon O'Brien; pp 51 OMK Design Ltd © Kinsman Associates; pp 7 left, 52, 87-89, 92-93 © AENA/Manuel Renau; pp 7 centre, 58- 69 © Matt Dubbe / images courtesy of Architectural Alliance; pp 71, 75-77 © MWAA; pp 72-74 © MWAA/ Photos Eric Taylor; pp 79-85 OMK Design Ltd © Kinsman Associates; pp 91 © Richard Rogers Partnership; pp 95, 120-127 © Berry Bros & Rudd; pp 97, 114, 116-118, 153, 155 © BAA Limited; pp 99, 196-201 Courtesy of JHP; pp 115, 119 © Alan Macdonald and Gail Collingburn from WH Smith PLC; pp 128-133, 156-159 © King Power International Group Company Limited; pp 94, 134-139 © Marshall Lightfoot; pp 6 centre, 140-151 © Business area Consumers, Amsterdam Airport, Schiphol/ Corporate Communications, Schiphol Group; p 154 © David Poultney/In-press; pp 160-163 © K & P Architects and Planners; pp 6 left, 164, 168-175 © Virgin Atlantic; pp 167, 186-189 © Barber Design Consultancy Ltd; pp 190-193, 195 © BAA photo library; pp 194, 208-215, 226, 227 courtesy of Mulberry; pp 194 © Big Pictures; pp 225, 227 © Carter design Group

FOREWORD

It was sixty years ago, soon after the end of the Second World War, that commercial airline travel really started to become a reality. Forty years ago, with the advent of mass tourism and growth of international business traffic, airports started on their inexorable pattern of growth. Twenty years ago, the airport retail revolution commenced.

In the early days, a cup of tea, a sandwich and a newspaper was all that was on offer. Now the best airports offer a massive choice, sophisticatedly targeted at the specifically identified passenger mix. With non-aviation revenues overtaking the traditional income streams, retail is now one of the key factors in the culture of the best airports. This new world has spawned a myriad of specialist businesses from architects to market researchers, publishers to retailers. The best in the world are forever analysing, developing and moving forward.

Even today, the truly enlightened airport operators, retailers and associated businesses are in a minority. The private sector has led the retail revolution; however, the dynamics of the airport industry are such that in most cases it is the public sector that operates airports. Although the world is changing, the majority of the key decision-makers in these airports come from a traditional operational aviation background. These airports tend to have much less financial incentive for profit and in many cases this colours their attitude to the importance of retail.

This, however, is missing the point; the benefits are not just about profit. Providing the best, most diverse, dynamic and comprehensive commercial facilities whilst also giving passengers value for money enhances the passenger experience and raises the airport's overall standing. We can all learn from the best. The future lies in innovation based on experience and knowledge, more enlightened airport management with a culture of experimentation and a deep understanding of the ever-changing world of airport retailing.

Robbie Gill
Managing Director, The Design Solution

PREFACE

This book was born many years ago in my mind and quite literally 'took off' with the rapid advancement and changes in the airports themselves. Airports offer a fascinating insight into how different cultures intermingle. There is sadness and there is joy as passengers leave and arrive, and all this happens in a confined space under one roof.

Much has been written about airport buildings, but to date this has been based primarily on the exterior 'look' and structure. To a certain extent this misses the point of what an airport is actually for and what goes on within it. The whole process is centred around the passenger – a person who may not even want to be there, but who is a captive audience within the airport travel system. The passenger's needs are great, and can range from easy-to-spot washroom facilities through to the retailing of luxury goods. Passengers themselves range from those on domestic flights who spend a relatively short time in the airport, to those who are there for hours awaiting a connecting flight. With the increasing requirement for airports to pay their way, 'design for business' is more critical than ever.

This book is not just about best practice in the wide variety of commercial situations; it is also about the creative protagonists and just how the situation arose in the first place. For example, the need for a chair that is not only designed to be comfortable to sit in but also to withstand violent abuse. For retailers it is about understanding just how different airports are from the high street or shopping mall. For the designers, architects and other creative people involved it requires not only engaging with the particular context and functionality of airport interior design, but also wilfully putting the commercial success of their solution at the very heart of what they do.

The book is about people, aspirations … and for the author it fulfils a personal ambition to show the magic of what goes on inside airports, behind closed arrival and departure doors.

LEFT Rejuve, Heathrow Airport Terminal 1. The entrance from the terminal's ground floor. A significant amount of glass has been used both to attract passengers and to create an open atmosphere.

INTRODUCTION

The French philosopher Roland Barthes once proclaimed the car as the modern equivalent of the great Gothic cathedral. If so, today's airports have become veritable temples to government and municipal egos – and that's without adding the 'signature architect's' name to the equation. In short, airports now have an iconic status attached to them, no longer shipping points to far-off places but cultural symbols indicating how a country, city or province positions itself. Airports themselves have become conduits for business and tourism. Not only do they offer the businessperson an efficient way of transport to clients' bases far away, but the airports themselves are commercial hubs for an area employing thousands of people in their operation. For some international cities such as London, the lack of possibility to expand size and therefore number of flights can actually limit the commercial success of that city. The bigger the airport becomes as demand grows, the more advanced the facilities will need to be. It is how the interior works that makes for an effective – or otherwise – airport terminal.

The last two decades have seen a massive expansion of the global air transport network. At a conference held in July 2006 by the Airports Council International (ACI), it was quoted that passenger numbers for the year 2005 were up considerably on the previous year at a growth percentage of 6.5 per cent – North America up 0.1 per cent, Europe up 3.6 per cent, the Asia Pacific countries up 7.5 per cent – with a 4 per cent rise of passenger traffic projected annually until the year 2020. This, as the President of the ACI mentioned, is already putting a severe strain on airports. China alone has an amortised passenger growth figure since 2001 of between seven and eight per cent and in 2002 it had 141 airports. This figure is projected to rise to 240 by 2010 – providing great potential for all concerned in the airport marketplace, which has gone from steady business and tourist use to daily commuting and the frequent-flyer leisure passenger. Consistent economic growth around the world has meant that there has been increased corporate and personal confidence in the future; this in turn has led to greater demand for more frequent flights on common routes and the flying public's desire for access to even more exotic locations. Global deregulation and the lifting of protection of main routes have meant that there has been an increase in new opportunities for what are now termed 'low-cost operators', so that flight ticket prices have fallen dramatically. This single act has caused European short-haul routes to expand both in flight numbers and also in the opening of new destinations, demanding the expansion of those airport terminals and the enhancement of their facilities.

There has of course also been 9/11, a cataclysmic event that threatened to derail not only the world's economy but also the whole genre of flight. Passenger numbers fell dramatically – an expected knee-jerk reaction – but fortunately passenger growth resumed relatively quickly considering the scale of this dreadful event. What it has meant is a complete re-think of the security arrangements within the airport structure and management. This is particularly applicable to the USA where the terminal interiors for their heavy domestic passenger traffic had to be immediately reconfigured to cope with the added pre-flight security measures. A passenger terminal has gone from being little more than a bus stop to a two-hour check-in scenario, with the resultant passenger queues and backlog. Human nature being what it is, the response has been to turn the negative into a positive. Passengers need services while they are in a 'hold' situation and one way of paying for the increased security costs is to expand the earning of commercial revenue. Airport operators, retailers and food and beverage providers have been quick to step up to the mark and both adapt and expand their offers for passengers, who now find themselves with time to spare as a consequence of changes in check-in times. Global passenger terminal operators such as the UK-based BAA are now taking on contracts to manage either the whole airport or certain terminals of airports

ABOVE Sydney Airport is the world's oldest continually operating commercial airport. A major hub for Quantas, it is also the busiest commercial airport in Australia and a major retail centre. In 2006, it handled in excess of 30 million passengers.

in the USA. Out of chaos has come calm, and a calm that has shown a rise in passenger spend and growth in commercial activities. This passenger 'holding' principle is new to the USA, Middle and Far East with the exception of Israel, although in Europe and particularly the UK it has been *de rigueur* for decades now. As a result the sophistication of airport interiors and how they manage the terrorist threat is quite comprehensive and understood by the travelling public, which is key for all commercial activities.

AIRPORTS AND PASSENGERS

There is a strange relationship between the passenger and the airport: a sense of foreboding when it comes to the flight – Will it be on time? Will the plane be clean? – and this without the anxiety of flying itself. Now couple this with the global perception that the product, be it a sandwich or a T-shirt, will be not only of poor quality but also expensive, and disgustingly so! It is easy to see what a tremendous task the airport has to perform – and, to be quite frank, it fails all too often. The passenger continues to believe that the terminal's facilities are priced at a higher level than the high street or shopping mall would charge. It is only the major commercial global operators such as BAA and the like who fully understand this, and have instigated a marketing structure, price promises and a very proactive commercial facilities programme. For most, reality has still not hit home.

Despite these reservations, passengers still flock to fly in their millions; and as global commercial markets open up, the need for new airports or the expansion of existing ones increases. One phenomenal example of this is China – more a continent than a country. China's own deregulation and opening-up of itself both politically and commercially has not been an easy path to take. What this has meant is a marketplace for the world, the need to be able to fly into various areas of China in order to stimulate commercial activity and therefore develop markets in manufacturing and services. Control of the airport expansion programme was initially divested to the regions but because of soaring costs has now been taken back to Beijing to coordinate. The very nature of airports as a tool for trade and cultural exchange makes them a prime opportunity for global commercial activity. There is a programme in place run by the Civil Aviation Administration of China that stipulates that there are over 150 airports either planned or being developed at present – all with the need for global products and services. This is a new business for China as its population have no history of mass travel either internationally or domestically, and all airports have to subscribe to verifiable international standards.

Other areas such as the Middle East and the Far East are similar in having very proactive airport-building programmes, and unlike Europe there is an abundance of space and no prospect of public backlash. In fact the enthusiasm for such places is very much part of the culture. Cities such as Dubai and countries like Oman have promoted themselves as tourist destinations. Figures supplied by ACI Europe show that Dubai International Airport had double-digit growth in passenger traffic for the year 2005 – up from 21.7 million in 2004 to 24.7 million in the year 2005. With this expansion has come a kind of segregation of airport types, and this sparks competition between airports. Europe has the three major 'hub' airports – a 'hub' airport being a 'fly into and fly on to' flight facility – and these are London Heathrow, Paris Charles-de-Gaulle and Frankfurt. These three are in direct competition as the 'hub' to fly to and from on an international basis. They also double up as domestic 'hubs' within their own countries. The much-needed expansion of all three is heavily censured by the public's environmental concerns. This throws up an anomaly: the public wants more flights and cheaper fares but objects to expansion in order to provide this service. This is very much a European scenario, with the increase of cheap 'no-frills' flights being coupled with the view that airport expansion is not good for the environment.

National airports have been the background to the flight industry. They offer all the major international routes complete with a good domestic structure to feed the growing number of regional airports. This scenario is the epitome of the USA which, because of its geographical location, has no real need for 'hub' operations, as its national airports are major destinations in themselves. There is an ever-increasing blurring of the edges between the major national airports and the burgeoning regional variety as these too offer an increasing number of international locations. This is particularly relevant to Europe, as the 'low-cost' operators favour regional airports as a base. Even with a cursory glance it is easy to see that airports have to evolve – which makes the interior masterplanning so important to their commercial life.

ARCHITECTURE AND DESIGN

Essentially, many of the world's older airports were conceived as municipal buildings. Dane County Regional Airport in Madison, Wisconsin is a good example of this, and still today retains that feel. In England, Gatwick Airport was about as 'municipal' as an airport could get. Its architect was appointed by the government, and the structure was a series of rectangular boxes with, as in the USA, long piers emanating outwards. No designer was appointed to work on the interiors of the earlier airports, their lighting and seating provision were basic, and there was very little in the way of activity, commercial or otherwise, in which the passenger could partake. A news stand with a very narrow range of printed matter; a café with a similarly limited and unappealing offering. It was simply not thought that the environment was important for the passenger's sake: here the planes and airlines were all that mattered.

The first thing to change was that airports across Europe and then the USA started to be designed by architects who saw them as a derivative of Modernist buildings, and a blossoming of creativity followed. Paris Charles de Gaulle, designed by Paul Andreu in 1965, is emblematic of this new era. Construction started in 1967 and with various updates the airport at Roissy has become iconic. Interiors were modern in approach; lights, seating and effective signage had finally entered the airport world – but not, however, commerciality. The 'municipal' element was still there in the form of airports being owned and run by governments who by nature have a habit of spending money rather than making it. There was however a major breakthrough that was to turn the use of design in airports into a full-blown race for successful commerce. This was the privatisation of the British Airports Authority by the government of the day. The Airports Act 1986 enabled BAA plc to be floated on the London Stock Exchange in July 1987, capitalised at £1,225 million. It was typical Thatcher – 'hive it off so it no longer costs us money although we will retain a stake in it.' The flotation was also unusual in that it had an income stream that was to decrease year on year, as its landing fee income was legally restricted. What is now BAA has turned the company's birth scenario on its head by employing architects and designers, turning the perception of the nature of an airport interior on its head and in the process posting profits into the hundreds of millions of pounds sterling. The commercial masterplanning of Gatwick Airport North Terminal in 1989 was an exercise in the combination of effective design and operator foresight, a most productive solution for any airport: every aspect was improved, with office space turned into passenger space, excellent terminal fit-outs, retail and catering offers to fit all tastes and pockets … and the development goes on. For BAA it is now a global business: the company secured its first American contract in 1992 with Pittsburgh Airport. From all this have come some quite staggering changes in airport interior design,

firmly anchored to the making of money and passenger gratification. Washington National Airport, for instance, has launched its glorious Architectural Enhancement Program for pure artistic gratification. Other airports, Madrid Barajas and Guangzhou Baiyun International, have turned the routine 'fit-out' into sound practical solutions for both finishes and seating. Whilst in the past airports have largely resembled one another both externally and internally, the idea of the interior 'sense of place' has now arrived and changed design thinking. Dane County Regional Airport in Wisconsin is a prime example – and this is not an international airport, but simply one that understands the benefits of pleasant surroundings.

The areas that are always close to a traveller's heart and pocket are food and drink together with retail, and it is here where design must pay. Amsterdam Schiphol Airport has found a total food and beverage solution that satisfies all passenger requirements. All the design and commercial solutions in this book represent what an airport is all about: serving the traveller. The more effective the architecture and design, the more successful the airport.

RETAIL

Around the globe, retail is not only the most important business but also one of the oldest. It is not difficult to see, then, just how important it is to an airport; in short it is the main earner for the operator and one in which it has to keep reinventing itself. One of the first innovations was Duty Free shopping, an anomaly that started because if a customer bought a product that was to be 'exported' with them to another country – or, in the USA, another state – the 'interior' tax was not applicable. This phenomenon, like so much in retail, had its early roots in America. Two Americans called Charles Feeney and Robert W Miller opened the Duty Free Corporation in Hong Kong in 1960. These Duty Free retail outlets have historically been owned and managed either by a concessionaire, as in the USA, or by the airport itself. What this did was to stimulate the idea of passengers spending money, which if they were going on holiday they would be doing anyway. For passengers travelling within Europe it all came to an end in 1999 when the EU levelled taxes between member states. The result was that duty had to be paid – but not tax, a fact of which a lot of European passengers remain unaware. The 'recommended retail pricing' structure also gave rise to airports having a perception of being a bit of a rip-off, an attitude that still prevails today amongst passengers.

Retail started to move on, especially in Europe: first local shops expanded to the high street, and then, as the high street became a global marketplace, so these brands – whether national brands such as WH Smith the newsagent and stationer, or global players like GAP – were attracted to the airports. Enter the retail masterplanner, a person who would completely reconfigure terminals into shopping malls. This process did not happen overnight; it took years and was a difficult creative and managerial task. Egos were at stake: the 'signature architect' of the airport did not want retail upsetting the harmonious space, and treated the application with disdain. The operating companies such as the UK's BAA plc also had to become retail savvy, and so hired retail management personnel to oversee the tortuous business. This new approach started in earnest in the early 1990s, and has now become an art form. Brands are positioned in terminals according to the socio-economic groupings of the footfall, and shops can merchandise their stores – all of which have open fronts – according to specific flights going out or coming in. There are also subtle differences between airside and landside retailing. Airports have become the global village of brands.

Passengers are only one market. There are others: the meeters and greeters – a small group – and the staff, totalling 18,000 people at London Gatwick, equivalent to a small town. This entire masterplanning encompasses and promotes the need for related services such as signage, lighting and seat positioning – not to mention marketing, which starts before you have entered the terminal. The airport outlet is a sophisticated retail cell, much more than its shopping-mall counterpart. It operates 24/7, has defined markets that change from hour to hour, and pays a rent according to turnover rather than the part of town in which it is located.

FOOD AND BEVERAGE

For many years the food and drink offering at most airports was very much like the retail scenario: pretty poor. Europe, with the exception of France but with particular reference to the UK, was backward compared to the USA. Customers at airports could expect to pay higher prices for lower quality than they would find elsewhere.

In many ways this particular airport marketplace has walked hand in hand with the retail masterplanning mentioned previously, although it involves a lot of subtle social and cultural differences. In the early days in Europe the airport had the traditional silver service restaurant; London's Heathrow Airport was a good example of this historic solution to feeding people. As times changed, airports became more open to different choices. Bars expanded with a limited 'snack' offer, and cafés began to sell more than just coffee. Then onto the scene came not just the brands, but also the American phenomenon of fast food. Bars, which have always had an importance in airports, started to be 'themed'; the Irish bar is a classic, but there are also wine bars, champagne bars and in England a first with the Caviar Bar. Like retail, catering is now global, and 'grazing', a concept which originated in the USA, is now endemic across the globe. Eating is not only a 'must-do' activity – it is fashionable, and so airports have started to attract specialist food and beverage providers. This not only upgrades the offer but gives the passenger a 'sense of place': 'I may be in an airport to yet another capital city, but at the moment I am having a locally caught and prepared seafood salad, with a glass of equally local wine.' Such attitudes are growing amongst passengers and give rise to considerable further scope within the airport marketplace. The tide has changed against fast food, health is on the march and the world could be your oyster.

LEISURE AND WELLBEING

Airport lounges and leisure areas are the new 'in places', and as such their design has to reflect their importance. Their roots stem from both overall passenger health concerns and the need to pass eight hours in a 'hub' airport awaiting a connecting flight. Airlines, particularly the global carriers with long-haul flight destinations, have for some time now been devising ways to pamper their customers – at the most basic level by developing on-board refresher packs built around hydrating the face after a long flight. British Airways have teamed up with the British skincare brand Molton Brown to supply their products to their own passengers. Virgin Atlantic have designed and built their own 'Clubhouses', facilities that offer food, drink, pool, music and massage, all part of the Virgin brand. This is not for all passenger groups, however, but strictly for the first-class frequent flyer, on whom the airline depends so much. From these tentative and rather cosmetic steps they have expanded into leisure and rest spaces, built into the airline's own area and not part of the general airport. How they operate varies greatly from airline to airline and is still a growth area.

'Hubs' are as competitive as any airline in wanting not only airline business but also passenger preference. It works like this: a frequent long-haul flyer may choose the connecting flight based on the facilities at the 'hub' airport – such as Singapore Changi Airport, often touted as a favourite with passengers – rather than the airline. Airlines may choose to fly into and out of an airport based on the same passenger preference – a chicken and egg situation. The Middle and Far East are fast developing ever-new facilities in order to attract both parties. This makes sound commercial sense, but the question is: how far can it all go? Space tends not to be a problem in these places, and they have a known timeframe in which the passenger will be free to indulge in whatever is on offer. The possibilities are endless; 21st-century technology is bound to play a part in future developments, and companies with innovative ideas and products will thrive.

As we can see, airports are not only complex places but also veritable temples to all who build and operate them, and who work to enhance the lives of passengers and staff alike. They are a wonder of the modern world.

PASSENGERS AND AIRPORTS

The 20th century was responsible for many things. One of the more positive and pleasurable of these was the development of the airport. Its origins are to be found in the essentially military establishment of the aerodrome – a grass landing strip with accompanying tin hut and control tower. Although some of the latter are now listed monuments, they sound jolly uncomfortable in today's terms. But from this tender start, the 'airport' evolved, based around plane and passenger. It has been an evolution of gargantuan proportions that has seen the globe shrink by the joining of world cultures to do business, exchange views, or simply to enjoy themselves. As a result the airport has attained a status of almost religious proportions – and here lies its complexity.

Passengers are people, are they not? So it should be relatively easy to comprehend behavioural patterns and commercial desires. This, I am afraid, is not necessarily so. There are passengers who are frequent flyers and there are some, quite a high proportion, who are first-time flyers. Then there are passengers who fly for business reasons, and others for whom it is purely leisure. Even 'leisure' has its subdivision from a point of flight variety. Do they fly 'schedule' or 'charter'? – two important but different markets. There is even a group of flyers who do not want to be in the airport at all, as they are being repatriated against their will. All these differing groups walk the streets of the world and shop in the malls, but put them together in an airport and you are faced with a more complex issue.

These passenger groups and their implications in terms of both design and provision of commercial services are at the very centre of how today's airport interiors are conceived, and for this reason an analysis of them begins this section. No detail is too small, and like life itself the prognosis is an ever-changing one. The case study on research carried out by Aéroports de Paris amply exemplifies just how much detail is required to understand even a fraction of the travelling public; here we focus on male spending and retail habits. Special attention has been made to the recent phenomenon of the 'low-cost passenger', as this particular group is having such a major impact on the provision of new regional airports as well as the expansion of national airport facilities.

ABOVE JFK Airport. Eero Saarinen's majestic design for the JFK Airport, a further stepping stone in airport style and construction.

LEFT Gatwick Airport. Great oaks from little acorns grow. Gatwick Airport today has expanded well beyond what this photograph shows, both in flight numbers and interior facilities.

Airports have now become temples to travel: famed architects create the most unusual shapes and forms. This has not happened by chance or in response to the simple need to have a bigger and better flight facility; politics, a nasty word even at the best of times, has been one of the major drivers. They are, after all, the gateway to a country – so why shouldn't politicians have their input? In the main this has been a productive element, especially in the developing countries and continents such as China and the Middle East. 'We must have the best and the most significant international building in our country, and by the way it's an airport.' This is not as silly as it sounds: airports are good for business, and in the case of 'hub' airports a government's desire to be kingpin of a region in the provision of global flight is understandable. The growth in this particular airport type continues apace, and for more reasons than mere financial gain and prestige. For Copenhagen International Airport to act as a hub is essential for a very large land area that does not have the population density normally associated with hub airport requirements. It is an interesting hub solution for a more basic need.

National airports remain at the very heart of passenger requirements, with business and leisure activities centred around them. These airports are also subject to important global events that for a very short period of time, normally just a few weeks, have the capacity to transform an airport. Such events include global sporting occasions like the Olympic Games and the World Cup. The airports have to transform themselves in two ways: they must be able to cope with the surge in traveller traffic, and also become beacons for the host country – a gateway to the country's brand. From this generally springs a complete overhaul of the airport for the future, as our case study on Barcelona Airport has found. It has put in progress a total internal and external remodelling of its terminals which, interestingly, its instigators have managed to align with an effective environmental support programme. It is a project of very significant proportions which on its own has the potential to 'show the way' for other airports across the world. Barcelona Airport is adventurous and cohesive in its future plans. There is also a hidden plus to the 'have-to' element of remodelling an airport for a major sporting event – the public are far less likely to be so vocal in their condemnation of airport expansion. It is after all a national event that their country will be judged upon long after the medals have been awarded.

Regional airports around the world are the very backbone of air travel support, especially as they can cater for the growing band of low-cost carriers. They can of course support a region's growing economy, and can serve passengers on a much more intimate level than either a hub or a national airport ever can. Both the UK and continental Europe have ever increasing car travel congestion. The ability of airport and entrepreneurial carriers to offer a virtual commuter service to different parts of the home country is a potential gold mine. With low-cost couriers, they can define how an airport will reshape itself to cope with the surge in passenger numbers. Bristol International Airport is an excellent example of how the development of its own popularity almost superseded its expansion plans. This is a very real problem when any expansion plans are either inflexible as a building programme for the future or the plans take so long to be approved. Fortunately for most – but certainly not all – regional airports around the world, an operator or owner with a long-term view stretching decades rather than years helps. Such is the situation at Bristol Airport, which makes it such an ideal case study on all counts.

The environment is a big issue for both airport operations and the carriers themselves. It has to be taken into account and made part of any export expansion remit, as in the case of Barcelona, but – and it is a very large 'but' – airports are huge earners for any country's economy. They are the very lifeblood of the global economy as shippers of both people and goods. Tens of thousands of people depend on them for a living, bringing commercial wealth and prosperity to the region in which the airport is located. A balance must be achieved, but it must be one that is clear and concise and will not take an age to reach.

LEFT Dubai International Airport. Dubai Airport represents the worldwide expansion of airports as a marketplace in their own right. The style is truly 'international'.

PASSENGERS, MEETERS AND GREETERS
CASE STUDY: MEN'S SHOPPING BEHAVIOUR IN AN AIRPORT

Research by: Aéroports de Paris, France

Travel of whatever kind, with the exception of the office commute, has always been a magical thing, a bit of an adventure. People even used to dress up for it! Those days have in essence passed and travel has become a lot more democratic, no longer the reserve of the affluent and socially connected. Holidays taken whether alone, with friends or as a family unit still have that touch of magic – a new country to visit or a child's first flight, it all adds up to excitement. Hollywood has long been a great exponent of using airports and passengers either arriving or departing as major emotional moments of a film. It is all gripping stuff, and is very important in today's airport life. Passengers, meeters and greeters are the key to everything that happens, for without them airports would simply be a cargo terminal for global trade.

What is critical for everyone concerned in the business of air travel, from the carriers to the designers of a point-of-sale unit, is to understand this important group of people and to design, serve, create and sell successfully to them. It is the same all over the world. To a certain extent there are benefits in providing a commercial offering to these people in that for a space of time, often known, they are enclosed in a box with nothing to do except wait for a plane to take off or land. Meeters and greeters are included in this equation

as in certain parts of the world they can be as many as two-dozen-strong per passenger.

When seeking to know who and what a passenger is, it is important to understand why that person is there in the first place. Add to this the type of carrier, ticket price paid and by whom, and ultimate destination and the picture can be pretty complex, if not daunting. There are however some clear groupings of passengers that emerge from these considerations. The businessperson is one such group: generally speaking a passenger travelling on a high-cost ticket and extremely time conscious. This passenger will have access to virtually all the commercial areas of an airport from business lounges through to the use of airport hotels for stopovers en route. He or she will also more than likely be a major client of the world's hub airports and therefore the facilities that they provide. Within this global group, nationality has to be taken into account, and this breaks down into one of three main groups – Europe, Asia-Pacific and the Americas – with Africa as a smaller player.

The leisure passenger will come from one of the three major demographic groups but is unlikely to want to use, or even to have access to, a business lounge. Depending on how adventurous the travel destinations are, however, they could still use a hub facility. This type of passenger

TOP Charles de Gaulle Airport. The new look retail area in terminal 2F, a bright and easy to access area.

BOTTOM Charles de Gaulle Airport. Here the graphic panels are French flowers on the way to the boarding gates.

ABOVE The graphic panels have been developed by the French artist Petika to signify all things French. Here the Mona Lisa is in the pathway between 2C and 2A at Charles de Gaulle Airport.

is also seasonal, although with the global ageing population this is starting to be a more level playing field, especially within Europe. An airport's facilities matter a great deal to this grouping, as in a sense when they leave their own home they are 'on holiday'. Shops, food and beverage and short-time leisure are all within the personal remit of the leisure passenger. It is up to the airport operator to ensure that the terminal is correctly master-planned, whilst it is the retailer's job to purvey exciting products and the task of the catering supplier to provide the right refreshment at the right time of both travel and day.

The last group is essentially confined to America. 'Hop on, hop off' has disappeared post-9/11, but 'low-cost' is in some ways not a very apt description of US domestic flights as the average passenger income on some of the carriers can be high. What this phenomenon has been able to do is to democratise even further the process of flight. Fares are cheap, 'no-frills' seems to be the byword and there is now a group of passengers who have actually changed their own lifestyles to accommodate the possibility of more frequent travel. To a certain extent this has gone hand in hand with the rapid development of regional air-

ports and the carriers that they have attracted.

Targeting and measuring all these groups has been the work of airport operators such as BAA plc, Host and others who can provide significant data and research to aid any commercial entity thinking of entering the airport marketplace. This has become the very backbone of selling to all passengers and helps all the parties concerned. Store designers, restaurateurs, leisure providers and airport fit-out companies can all use this crucial information in their planning and implementation process. It is a very valuable business tool indeed.

A key example of this kind of research took place at the beginning of 2006 when Aéroports de Paris conducted the first ethnographic study about men's buying behaviour in an airport. The survey was carried out with the support of Added Value Agency and sociologist Stéphane Chevrier, a travel and research director at the University of Rennes.

This extensive investigation proved just how important the male passenger is to an airport, especially when travelling alone. In the year 2005, 50 million men travelled though Parisian airports (63 per cent of total passengers). They spent on average 43 euros in the airport boutiques – 30 per cent more than women. The single male passenger is a more autonomous person compared with when travelling with a female companion or family. He takes time to learn how to shop, compare and try out, and purchases his own rather than in everyday life relying on his companion. He seeks information about a wider variety of topics and services – an interesting example being that male passengers found lingerie and undergarment shops particularly attractive. What was also shown was that the shopping experience was thorough and exhaustive – completely different from male urban shopping habits. What is more, the male passenger is quite prepared to 'waste time' and sees airport shopping as part of a relaxation process.

Only 1 per cent of men would enter a perfume shop on the high street, whilst at an airport the figure rises to 21 per cent. They are also spenders: 52 per cent of the male passengers visited boutiques and one third of this number departed with at least one purchase. A man spends on average 7 euros more than his female counterpart and 60 per cent of the purchases show that the man has a hedonistic dimension to his shopping, as these are items for him and not gifts. Purchases tend to focus on duty-free products such as alcohol, perfumes, designer clothing and accessories, and he often buys in quantity to maximise the 'deal'.

Who are these male spendthrifts? According to the survey they are largely from the upper socio-professional categories: businessmen, engineers, high-level technicians and professionals of every nationality. What this research also found is that when a male passenger is accompanied, he takes charge of all the practical matters of flying but reverts to 'companion' status, leaving all other decisions on whether to enter a shop or purchase to his female partner.

Because of the high percentage of male passengers, this piece of research has helped to shape Aéroports de Paris's thinking on retail, as Pascal Bourgue, Marketing, Retail and Communications Director, comments: 'Their perception of the airport and their expectations are determining criteria for formulating and constantly adjusting our offer of services at our Paris airports.'

This is a very good example of just how far airports and their operators will go in determining what services they should be providing. It also gives an insight for all participants in the creative process on how to design for and communicate to specific passengers.

LEFT A male domain! The 'Men's Lounge' at Charles de Gaulle Airport offers male pampering products in a very brightly lit environment, thereby facilitating easy choice.
RIGHT Point-of-sale displays offer a wide range of men's favourite products together with on-shelf travel promotions.

INTERNATIONAL HUB AIRPORTS

CASE STUDY: COPENHAGEN INTERNATIONAL AIRPORT, DENMARK

Operator: Copenhagen Airports A/S, Denmark

It is hard to say what is the most important factor driving the growing business of airport expansion. All business is now truly global, and despite the development of video conferencing and all forms of techno-gadgetry, there is still the need for face-to-face meetings. Soon we will have to redefine the term 'low-cost carriers' as their importance is now so large. Carriers such as British Airways and Virgin have all set up their own low-cost operations to capture a segment of this growing market. Airports themselves need to attract both carriers and passengers, and none more so than the 'hub' variety.

This is fast becoming a very cut-throat marketplace, especially in the Middle and Far East. Hong Kong International Airport, the most traditional of all hubs, has a $4.5 billion (US dollars) airport enhancement investment programme in its attempt to stay ahead of its near competitors. On the other hand, the hub status of Copenhagen International Airport has arisen essentially out of its geographical location rather than competitive commercial practice, and it is not the size of other hub operations. In fact it is minuscule by comparison, with only 20 million passengers per year (2005) – whilst for most hub airports the figure is in excess of 50 million. Nevertheless, for Scandinavia it is a very important facility, and one which can only grow in its influence for business as well as leisure.

Copenhagen Airports A/S, listed on the Copenhagen Exchange, is no provincial operator. Its sphere of influence in its management and corporate strategy is global. Airports such as Newcastle International in England, Hainan Meilan in China and those of ASUR (Aeropuertos del Sureste de México) in Mexico have all benefited from investment and management from Copenhagen Airports A/S.

Despite its relatively small size in relation to other hubs, Copenhagen Airport is the largest airport facility in Scandinavia and is growing fast. Passenger figures for 2005 rose by 5 per cent compared with 2004; that is, by an extra million flyers. The interest lies, however, in the breakdown of passenger figures, which show how central the airport's hub status is to this growth. The number of transfer/transit passengers makes up 33.4 per cent of the departing passenger figures, and the number of international passengers rose by 5.1 per cent in the same period. The 'local' passenger routes to the Nordic countries have only 0.3 per cent growth. As with other airports, low-cost traffic is growing fast, and in 2005 this market made up 10 per cent of total passenger numbers, with a 10.5 per cent rise on the previous year.

As part of the strategy for managing Copenhagen International Airport there has been a steady programme of outsourcing to professional

ABOVE Pier C in Terminal 3, a non-Schengen area designed by Danish architects Holm & Grut.

LEFT Transfer desks and baggage handling all in one place. The marble floor and glazed roof provide a relaxed feel and the chairs are all equipped with wireless access.

operators in order to promote growth. Hotels, restaurants, shops and even parking facilities have all been outsourced, leaving the operating body to negotiate contracts and leasing of premises and land to third parties. In today's commercial marketplace this makes sound financial sense, for you cannot be all things to all people. This commercial zone is 10,000 square metres in area and consists of 11 duty and tax-free shops together with 38 specialist shops, restaurants and bars, a significant hub offer for only 20 million passengers.

As the southernmost major airport in Scandinavia and the hub of the region, Copenhagen Airport operates air traffic to and from Scandinavia and the Baltic. The large geographical distances in Norway and Sweden and the relatively low population density in these areas make Copenhagen International Airport the natural airport for transfer traffic. Intra-European traffic in particular is anchored in the passenger base in Øresund region, whilst transatlantic and Asian traffic comes from the Nordic countries and from northern Germany. The fact that the Scandinavian carrier SAS uses Copenhagen as its natural hub is very fortuitous as it is a member of

the important Star Alliance, a network of 16 international airlines that fly to a total of 795 airports in 139 countries. For Copenhagen there are direct connections in 132 destinations worldwide.

What makes Copenhagen such an effective and pleasant hub operator is the provision of facilities in the terminals. Special attention was paid two years ago to upgrading the terminals due to an increase in security requirements. Facilities for the less able and children are particularly good, and with 22,000 employees working in the many and various companies that provide the service mantle for the airport, it is no wonder that it is consistently one of the highest ranked airports in the world. It is not an airport to rest on its laurels, as an airport spokesperson commented: 'Copenhagen is a natural geographic hub, but due to the expansion in low-cost airlines in Scandinavia we still have to improve the transfer concept, as more passengers from the other Scandinavian countries tend to fly direct instead of transferring via Copenhagen.'

The airport has strong growth potential and more capacity will be needed. There is also the factor that the region's economy is both strong

LEFT The highly impressive shopping mall rising three levels, designed by Vilhelm Lauritzen.

RIGHT A panoramic view of the Terminal 3 check-in area complete with a bronze sculpture by the artist Hanne Varming of *Two Girls in the Airport*, a sculpture inspired by two similar girls in the same pose in Paris.

OVERLEAF The Eyecon Bar in Terminal 2, designed by Morten Hedegaard: a combined restaurant and bar facility where a passenger can enjoy tapas as well as a drink.

TOP LEFT The Caviar House is run by different concessionaires and is located in Terminal 3. It is a shop and a bar built into one area complete with a café.

BOTTOM LEFT The FineFood area selling Danish specialities, designed by Sussi Fischer.

BELOW Copenhagen's tax-free shopping area of 2,500 square metres, situated in Terminal 2 airside.

and growing, and this will add more pressure for airport expansion. What this hub airport offers probably more than most international hubs is ease of transfer. It is a relatively small hub so transferring is not seen as a major task to be conquered. The airport is spacious with both departure gates and facilities 'just around the corner' from each other. It has a relaxed and efficient atmosphere, and if you are about to spend eight hours on a plane or a few hours awaiting a connection, this is important. As a hub built out of geographical necessity rather than financial dexterity, as some of the others appear to be, the future of Copenhagen International Airport will be most interesting to follow.

ABOVE The ground-floor area rising to the first floor at Pier C.

RIGHT The ground-floor area at Pier A with an abstact mosaic in marble and granite by the Danish artist Jørn Larsen.

ABOVE LEFT The Terminal 3 check-in area, designed by Vilhelm Lauritzen, is four storeys high and built in granite, glass, aluminium and steel.

ABOVE RIGHT The rail connection point below Terminal 3 is designed and built in white travertine marble and granite. The glazed roof enhances the open look and a wall graphic signifying travel.

MAJOR NATIONAL AIRPORTS

CASE STUDY: BARCELONA AIRPORT, SPAIN

Operator: AENA, Spain

National airports the world over are the very lifeblood for both the business and tourist worlds. They are the destination places. Regional airports could have been overlooked both in relation to the necessary investment and in terms of interest from airline operators; but fortunately they have not – investment has driven new airline opportunities. A quick look at the continent of China with over 160 new airports planned or under development ably demonstrates the vibrancy of national airports.

One such airport is Spain's Barcelona Airport, the history of which reminds us of how countries' national airports grew out of nothing. It dates back to 1916 when it merely consisted of a 600-metre-long runway on a farm called La Volatería. Two years later it had its first international flight with a plane en route to Monaco. Iberia, the flagship Spanish carrier, had by 1927 set up a regular service from Barcelona to Madrid, a major move that was to develop both cities' commercial activities and was for its time ahead of the European game. By 1963 the airport had passed the million-passenger mark and in 1968 a new terminal was built, complete with a Joan Miró mural for the building – the first art in airports? Barcelona Airport achieved five million passengers by 1977 and in 1990 a separate organisation named AENA

(Aeropuertos Españoles y Navegación Aérea) was set up to both run and manage all the Spanish airports. Expansion was rapid: in 1997 the airport topped 15 million passengers and in 1999 AENA produced an airport masterplan called 'The Barcelona Plan' which was to manage the tremendous changes and developments of the airport until 2015. This brief synopsis of Barcelona's history is important because it is a transglobal activity for national airports. In Barcelona's case it is one of the best planned and most adventurous of its kind, for not only does it address the building envelope, but it also takes into consideration the total transport needs of Barcelona and potential ill effects on the environment. It is truly holistic in its thinking, planning and execution.

Barcelona today is at the heart of an economic development area as well as a tourism hot spot. Since the Olympic Games in 1992 Barcelona Airport has doubled its passenger traffic. This rapid growth brought about by commerce and tourism could not be sustained without a fundamental redevelopment of the existing airport. The Barcelona Plan is going to create an airport with a capacity of 40 million passengers. In the plan itself there are some sound figures for such an adventurous building programme. Within a three-hour travel timeframe there are 20 million inhabitants,

ABOVE Barcelona Airport. Interior view of the airport showing a food and beverage outlet.

ABOVE Barcelona Airport. A view of the airport at night.

and within the European Union business framework it ranks seventh most attractive city to do business in – and that is not because of the weather! From 1994 to 2004 Barcelona Airport had a growth in passenger numbers of 8.56 per cent, making it the second fastest growing European airport, and it has over the last few years been a winner of the 'Best Airport Award' from the publication *Business Travel World*, as well as gaining a similar award from *Condé Nast Traveller*. These two magazines represent both commerce and the public, so it is praise indeed. There are two elements to the Barcelona Plan: the first is to upgrade the existing facilities, and the second is to design and build new ones that will double the airport's capacity. Part of the plan is to lay another runway, bringing the airport's total to three. Normally to build in another runway as part of a masterplan would risk wrecking the whole projected programme, as public protest in the European Union over the expansion of airports is now commonplace. Here the whole area, commerce, and the public were viewed as part of the programme, so the planned development of the airport was not only seen as beneficial, but was welcomed.

One of the most adventurous elements of the masterplan is the creation of the new South Terminal, a building over five floors and 525,500

square metres with a capacity to process 25 million passengers. It is big! What this building does is to bring check-in, boarding, railway systems, buses and car parking all under one roof. From the passenger use perspective it is also a very friendly building: level changes are kept to a minimum and even these will be built in such a way that the less able passenger will find them easy to use. The plans show large open spaces, now *de rigueur* for any new terminal build – areas well lit by natural light and crystal facades – but probably the best element of all is that despite its size the passengers will only need to walk short distances between services. The project revolves around four key pieces: a transportation hub, a logistical centre, a service centre and an architecturally relevant building designed to handle an enormous number of passengers. There are also 'future' plans to build a rooftop hotel/convention centre and gardens.

Within the period 2000–2008 there are 80 projects of differing size being built. The renovation of Terminal B will see a new retail area with more shops and services, a redevelopment and expanded baggage reclaim facility and additional car parks. All this is going on while passenger traffic increases and the airport remains open as usual.

ABOVE AND OPPOSITE RIGHT Barcelona Airport. The new entrance to the airport with the air traffic control tower behind it.

Arrivals foyer

Part of the Barcelona Plan is the very rigorous 'Environmental Action Plan', with an investment of over 100 million euros. It is significant because it treats people, animals, culture and protection as one. There is an Aeronautical Culture Centre together with a Wildlife Recovery Centre. Airports are often seen as separate from both the immediate environs and the non-passenger public. At Barcelona Airport that idea is discarded; it is all-embracing and that is the added-value success. On a purely economic footing, 4,000 new jobs will be created as a result of the expansion, so that when the redevelopment is complete the airport will employ a total of some 40,000. Not bad for the local area economy or the efficiency of a national airport.

ABOVE Barcelona Airport. Aerial view showing just how close the airport is to the Mediterranean Sea.

TOP LEFT Barcelona Airport. The passenger piers with Spain's national airline Iberia's planes in the foreground.

BOTTOM LEFT Barcelona Airport. A view of Barcelona National Airport airside.

THE RISE OF REGIONAL AIRPORTS
CASE STUDY: BRISTOL INTERNATIONAL AIRPORT, UK

Owners: Macquarie Bank, Australia; Grupo Ferrovial, Spain

Regional airports the world over have been gaining in importance for several years now for a wide variety of reasons. For China they are an essential way of linking the continent together and providing a network for people involved in international business there. In Europe they are 'destination' airports for both tourism and business and are key to the ever-burgeoning low-cost flight operators. Bristol International Airport in the UK is an excellent example of the reasons for the growing importance of regional airports.

In 2005 Bristol Airport celebrated 75 years in existence and the last 10 to 15 years have seen massive route development activity. Bristol and its environs form a major commercial centre and as such the UK government has nominated it one of its six core cities. Its catchment area has a potential seven million airport users. Where the airport is situated is also critical as not only is it just six miles from the city centre, but also at the crossroads of a major motorway complex. Transport to the city centre is excellent as it has a designated bus and train service. The companies within its locale such as IT and the largest aerospace organisations have meant that the population are both affluent and have a high level of car ownership. Passenger levels in 1996 were 1.5 million; by 2006 they were 5.5 million and rising. Destinations have grown to 114

across 28 countries and Bristol is also important as an 'inbound' location for both business and tourism. One of the most interesting areas of growth has been in UK domestic destinations, with Bristol now servicing 17 airports. This growth within the UK is based on two aspects that are in fact linked: one is lack of travel time for the business community and the other is the lack of an adequate road network within the UK as successive governments have failed to respond to the need for its expansion.

All this has meant that the airport has had to grow and develop significantly in recent years. In March 2000 a brand new terminal was built to cope with the then 2 million passengers. This coincided with a complete re-branding of the airport to 'International', in keeping with the service it provided. Go, the airline taken over by Easyjet, made Bristol its first base outside London's four airports. This was based on the new terminal space and facilities and allowed them to develop further their range of destinations, which in turn led to increased passenger numbers. The interesting element of the new airport was that it was first planned back in the 1990s but, predictably, was subject to an ongoing public enquiry, which delayed the construction so much that it was redesigned four times in the interim to get it up to

TOP RIGHT Bristol International Airport. Bar des Voyageurs, a balcony bar complete with views of the airfield.

BOTTOM RIGHT Bristol International Airport. The business lounge, with the luxury of carpet, easy chairs and informal side tables for computer or drinks.

the four million-passenger capacity that was then required. The last three years have seen significant steps to expand the footprint area, particularly for check-in desk requirement and baggage reclaim facilities. What is quite obvious is that the delays have had a detrimental effect on how Bristol International Airport can carry out its business.

The airport's owners have quite rightly resolved to produce a proper masterplan in order to develop the facilities for the years to come. It is a blueprint for the future. Bristol now has 10 per cent year-on-year growth and is predicting eight to nine million passengers by 2015 and 10 to 12 million by the year 2030. The masterplan calls for additional gates, an on-site hotel and an increase in car-parking provision.

Two results of running the redevelopment scheme whilst continuing with 'business as usual' in the existing airport building have been the

need to create extra passenger space and expansion of the much-needed revenue stream obtained out of retail and food and beverage facilities. The airport now has a mezzanine floor, which has increased the space significantly. A four-million-pound retail and catering investment programme has now been completed which has included not only the expansion of space for brands already operating within the airport, but also the arrival of new operators. Nuance has been able to double its Duty Free area together with major expansion programmes for other retailers such WH Smith and Tie Rack. Bristol has attracted new brands like Claire's Accessories and Superdrug.

Catering facilities have also been expanded, with the introduction of the UK brands Subway, Ritazza, Starbucks and local operator Soho Coffee Company. A million-pound investment in Echo Bar

ABOVE Aircraft parked at terminal.

BELOW Bristol International Airport. A detail of the standard of business lounge seating that now has to be provided in any lounge.

has provided a much-needed extended food and bar selection, which brings a more sophisticated offer to the airport. In all there are now eight different catering units across both the landside and airside areas of the airport. Since the airport has a very high business usage, the business facilities – including the lounges – have been expanded, as this passenger grouping is seen by the airport's operators as crucial to their development plans.

What has certainly assisted the airport's expansion plans is the fact that it is a government-nominated 'core city'. This has enabled it to bring itself into the planned city developments as a participant. The Greater Bristol Strategic Transport Study is a good example of this. Self-promotion is also very high on the airport's plans and has helped to develop all the facilities as the terminal has expanded. For the future the terminal will have a fast-track operation for check-in and individual check-in facilities for parties and groups.

Bristol International Airport is typical of an expanding regional airport. The fact that it has as its owners companies wishing to invest up to £50 million over the next five years amply shows the potential for such airports. Passengers and the flight industry alike now perceive them as a much-needed alternative to the major national and international 'hubs'.

TOP LEFT Bristol International Airport. Soho Coffee Company exemplifies the latest style of 'catering on display' – lighting overhead that illuminates the food offer below in an assumed 'natural' way, enhanced by the natural wood floor.

BOTTOM LEFT Bristol International Airport. The 'technology' shop complete with international consumer white-goods brands. This open-style concept of airport retailing with its easy-to-walk-through space is now endemic in the modern airport retailing environment.

RIGHT The very elegant Bristol Airport Control Tower.

ARCHITECTURE AND DESIGN

The rise of the use of architecture and design has over the last 50 years been phenomenal with regard to all things 'airport'. Where there was once a field and a tent now stands an architectural structure of vast proportions, symbolic of today's life. From canvas have come brick, concrete, steel, wood and the ubiquitous use of glass. Airports are truly shining examples of man's creativeness and commercial endeavour. Where has it all come from – for it must have its roots in something? Airports are 'passenger terminals' and in the international publication *Passenger Terminal World* it is easy to see the extent to which the various types of terminals – be they for air, rail or sea – are inspired by one another. They all have a similar customer base and they are all providing 'travel'. The great stations of Europe and America have provided the backdrop for the development of modern airports; some of them have even had the same commissioning body. Where airports differ from other terminals is in scale and location, a necessity born out of the sheer number of passengers. They also have to embody the phrase 'all things to all people': the architecture and design input has to cater for this but thankfully in segments. This element alone – the democratisation of flight – has led to new airports in the developing world, expansion of national ones and massive redevelopment of regional facilities, all with the use of advancing architecture and design methodology.

The whole world with few exceptions has been advancing as global business has expanded. China was and is becoming one of the most important economic powers. But then there was 9/11, an event that shook the world to its very core. As has already been mentioned, the air travel industry was the first to suffer – not just in the immediate, although thankfully short, downtime in air traffic, but also in terms of the resultant changes in how airports needed to be internally planned and designed. In America airports had become virtual 'bus stops' with no need for vast areas allocated to 'security'. Overnight this all changed, creating havoc for both passenger and airport operator. Europe was not so affected, as security for most countries had always been an issue. Airport operators in America working with their appointed architects and designers started to radically overhaul the interior space of airports and see the potential of commerce. Airports now have to pay their own way!

ABOVE Guangzhou Baiyun International Airport. The 'Trax' system in a multiple configuration format based on a two-chair, three-chair and four-chair configuration.

LEFT Venice Marco Polo International Airport. Venice has many bridges, but none quite like the neon-lit bridge leading to the departure level approaching the airport.

ABOVE Madrid Barajas International Airport.
The ceiling and terminal at first-floor level.

This now endemic commercial activity in airports has thrown up one key problem: the majority of airports were never designed to provide retail, food and beverage let alone wellbeing clinics. They, by the sheer force of financial necessity, have had to be re-planned, remodelled and rebooted into the 21st century. This in itself throws up 'creative' problems. The architect who designs the airport as a structure has historically not bothered about commercial space in the interior; in fact some practices have been extremely negative towards what they see as an indirect influence on their work. 'We design *airports*!' has often been the cry! Fortunately strong airport operators with shareholders to answer to hold no truck with creative egos and have quite literally forced architects, designers and everybody involved in the commercialisation of airport interiors to work as a 'partnership'. Not an easy task … but it works, because from this has now come a new airport building system that requires any proposal to have a partnership of both exterior and interior architects combined with the customary structural engineers. This is, and will be for some years to come, the basis of even more inspirational airports, structures that remain striking together with interiors that embolden that sense of commercial activity. We live in exciting times!

With the dramatic expansion of commerce within passenger terminals has come the need for well-thought-out design solutions, and this becomes more and more important the larger the airport. For large terminals there need to be better messaging systems for passengers, as the time it takes somebody to walk or negotiate from entrance to gate can be a long and difficult journey if not handled in an imaginative way. Hopefully it should be subliminal with the minimum of direct messaging.

Venice Airport has the benefit of being a new-build project and one in which the two architectural practices worked in harmony in creating an interior that puts the passenger at ease the moment he or she enters the terminal. With flight information at the entrance, you can almost feel the travel anxiety falling away! After that there is a clear hierarchy of terminal signage based on the less-is-more principle. It neither invades the space nor clutters the traveller's mind. This might seem simple but very few airports do it successfully, preferring a barrage of signs, layer upon layer, and turning the area into a veritable bazaar.

The public the world over are often very quick to criticise any new building. Airports are easy targets as they are both large and media visible. 'All airports look the same, you could be anywhere in the world' is a view frequently expressed. This is to denigrate the many subtle or sometimes not-so-subtle architectural and material features now being built into new and redeveloped airports. McCarran International Airport, Las Vegas *is* Las Vegas, but then there is Dane County Regional Airport in a style all of its own – a style which could be described as 'Prairie School'. Here the use of what is now termed 'sense of place' has been used in a most creative manner in the architecture of the building inside and out and in the use of materials. Its anchor is firmly resting in the history of the surrounding area. This airport has taken this genre and extended it; far from being a period piece it will be seen as iconic and of course it is admired both by passengers and by the local Madison population.

From 'sense of place' to Washington National Airport's Architectural Enhancement Program – the two are in essence linked by the creation of a treat both practical and visual. The use of American modern master artists together with all types of craftspeople has created an environment that is not art as an add-on, but art as an integral part of the terminal. The architect and airport authority encouraged artists to work outside of their normal craft, to go where they have not gone before, and the result is far beyond the word 'enhancement'. It goes back to an era where artists and architects worked together to create buildings rather than going their own separate and often non-integrated ways.

With the rapid change in airport interiors, not to mention expansion of the same, has come the pressing need for well-designed and lasting fit-out programmes. Painted walls and Granddad's chair to sit in is no longer the scene. For 'chairs' read 'seating systems' that can cope with abuse as well as different cultural requirements and yet still look sculptural. Steel and aluminium have replaced paint, born out of the need for practical lifetime expectations and ease of maintenance. Ceilings and lighting now have to cope with vigorous global standards that address both safety concerns and environmental issues. The design and subsequent implementation of airport interior fit-outs requires a very wide variety of solutions. It is also a growing market employing a very broad range of specialists. From shops to bars, from lifts to check-in counters, good design is being used. All this benefits the passenger and a happy passenger is a potential client for all that is on offer.

Even in this brief introduction it is not hard to see just how important architecture and design are for an airport. Here are fine examples, best practice and interesting solutions. Unfortunately they are not necessarily typical of the airport world, but are shown to indicate what it could be like.

AIRPORT SIGNAGE

CASE STUDY: VENICE MARCO POLO INTERNATIONAL AIRPORT, ITALY

Architects: Studio Architetto Mar, Venice, Italy; JHP Design, London, UK

Signs are hazardous to your health! Wherever you go – supermarket, sports stadium, and especially the road system – there are signs. These are devoid of clarity, hierarchy and even logical information; they seem to have been put there in an appliqué fashion, one on top of the other with the expectation that travelling in a car at medium speed you can take in up to six colours and 12 font sizes on anything up to six boards. This is before the ubiquitous road maintenance signs! In short nobody can take in that amount of visual clutter. What is being described is a global problem that has come about by expansion, whether it is new offers in a retail store or a new town or facility off a major highway. Signs are put upon signs with the expectation that they will be read and understood. If this scenario enters an airport interior – and all too often it does – then it can be even more stressful. The travelling public have very logical desires for information, they are our personal hierarchy if you like, and need to be firstly understood and then designed for. Where is check-in? Is the plane on time? Where are the toilets? – all prerequisites for passengers and meeters and greeters alike. It is a stressful time and immediate information is required. For a new-build airport there is no excuse not to get it right; for the world's expanding airports there needs to

be rigorous thought and planning as terminals evolve and more facilities are built in. Critical to all this is to have a working partnership between terminal operator, retail masterplanner and any architects and designers involved. Failure to have this can lead to a loss of cohesive information.

Venice Marco Polo International Airport, completed in 2002, is located next to the old airport which now exists as a cargo hold. The overall design provides not only an elegant vista over the lagoon for arriving passengers, but has its architectural style firmly anchored in Italian tradition. The airport building was designed by the architects Studio Mar, a major Italian practice known for significant public works such as hospitals, schools and other airports in Italy; whilst the interior masterplanning was conceived by JHP Design, a UK-based commercial design consultancy that has projects such as Zurich, Hong Kong and Bangkok airports, and is currently working on Shanghai Hong Qiao Airport ahead of the 2008 Beijing Olympic Games. JHP and the airport authority worked together to produce a signage information system, simple in its hierarchy – what the passenger needs to see first and so on, and how it is built into both the airport interior fit-out and retail, food and beverage facility. It works very much on a less-is-more principle so that in some

TOP Venice Marco Polo International Airport. What clarity! Clear, simple signs in an almost minimalist arena with only the coffee shop acting as a focal point.

MIDDLE Venice Marco Polo International Airport. The airport's 'reception', featuring the most important sign found in an airport: you enter and immediately you are put at ease by the flight information board that you cannot miss. It helps that it is a most attractive sign as well. This positioning assists both passenger flow and wayfinding in one simple shot.

BOTTOM Venice Marco Polo International Airport. Here the 'hub' signage has taken a retail negative – a wall rather than a window or open space – and turned it into a successful branding application.

elements the signage becomes almost subliminal for the passengers in the terminal.

One big advantage is that this airport was a new-build project so that all parties concerned had a blank canvas on which to work. Not so much reinventing the wheel, but contemporising and clarifying. As it is most important, directional signage came first, designed by both architectural practices as a joint project. Following on from this came the advertising signage that is based around the retail and catering offer. Here again, not only did it have to be clear and simple but it had to 'brand' the shops that are run by the airport authority in such a way that they did not look like a typical airport shop but a retail brand in its own right. Upon entering the airport through the single entry point, all the flight information is displayed on a central bank in the check-in area. All the much-needed and potentially stressful information at the passenger's first point of call! Directional signage has been given clarity of font together with various size levels to the system, which operate in a box principle. Here the hierarchy complements the system in that there are a variety of box sizes working with the information supplied.

The signage system operates out of a family of colours that further emphasise importance to the passenger. Numbers for the check-in bays are yellow out of black, as are all the other flight-related signs such as toilets, police and medical facilities. Non-flight information is produced in a simple white out of black format. It is worth noting that both these colour combinations work especially well for people with limited eyesight. The pictograms have been tweaked to complement the font and keep them contemporary but not brand new. What is clear is that none of the signage systems compete with each other or get in each other's way. One major reason for the success of this project is that it is also integral to the airport's fit-out, rather than being layered over the top. Where applicable, signs have been incorporated into the airport wall modular panel system, which not only cuts clutter physically but also means that a great deal of thought has to go into the correct positioning of each and every sign. There is of course the aesthetic benefit to this kind of sign application – it fits the architecture of the building as well, a quality that is not often seen even in retail parks!

The airport manages two different retail units within its own commercial remit: the concessionaire and the independent retailer. This could easily result in visual mayhem, but here a framework has been worked out and stuck to. All the airport's own brands have been developed to have a totally independent look from the point of signage so that they appear more 'high street' than 'airport shop'. One obvious visual element is that these retail signs are integral both to the architectural interior fit-out and to the shop's retail fit-out, a surprisingly holistic visual treat. The stand-alone retailers in the concessionaire space encompass quality purveyors Culto Caffè, a coffee and chocolate shop, and Bottega dei Sapori, selling local food, wine and spirits. Once again their own shop signage falls within the framework remit due in part to guidance given by JHP and working together on the 'look'.

Retail is full of illumination and technological wizardry, unfortunately along the lines of the mistaken idea that brightest is best. In this airport the illumination signage is harmonious rather than garish, and is used to enhance the message, be it a retail one or airport related. What is evident in the Venice Marco Polo International Airport is that the two architectural practices together with the various building parties worked together from the outset to ensure that every single element complemented every other, was harmonious to the eye and as a result the comfort level for the passengers is high and any stress caused by travelling is kept to a minimum. Steve Collis, Managing Director of JHP London, sums up the ethos of airport signage: 'You are on a journey at an airport so the signage has to be clear and take you on that journey through the airport. It must not be intrusive but be as clear as possible: that way it benefits everybody.'

ABOVE LEFT Venice Marco Polo International Airport. The signage for Venetia Studium, a graphic that echoes the merchandise being sold – authentic Venetian products.

ABOVE CENTRE Venice Marco Polo International Airport. The Travel Retail is a 463-square-metre store. Branding for cosmetic companies is paramount, and here it is both clear and controlled by the use of panels – a tried and trusted method, so why change it?

ABOVE RIGHT Venice Marco Polo International Airport. The large Duty Free retail offer is run by the airport's own retail company Airport Elite. This area successfully deals with the entire individual branding issues that are a Duty Free shop.

LEFT Venice Marco Polo International Airport. Here the Bottega dei Sapori graphic on the counter back echoes the entrance signage. Interestingly the entrance sign is on both sides of the entrance/ exit.

SENSE OF PLACE DESIGN

CASE STUDY: DANE COUNTY REGIONAL AIRPORT, MADISON, WISCONSIN, USA

Architect: Architectural Alliance, Minneapolis, USA

'Sense of place' architecture or design is one of the latest creative nuances to be fully exploited in passenger terminals and airports in particular. It can also come in various guises. Boston Logan International Airport, a major international US airport, has traded upon its local materials as a building tool together with seafood as a major influence in its food and beverage offer, which extends to a 'carry on' facility for the local delicacy, shellfish. It is a way of remembering where you have been in a most relaxed manner: that of eating.

Airports are often criticised for being nondescript clones of one another: 'You could be anywhere' is the passengers' cry. Advances in architectural thinking combined with new building technology now allow the creation of temples to travel, but even here there is often no anchor to where the airport actually is, no sense of place. Airports are gateways to a country or region, and as such why should they not reflect the local culture, surroundings and materials? They are after all on the doorstep and can flag up to the traveller just what he or she is going to experience. Working in reverse, it could be the last experience of the locale so why not imbue the atmosphere with the true nuance of the area? It could just be uplifting after a work-filled day. This 'sense of place' needs to be fully integrated into any airport masterplanning

and design. While new airports are rather thin on the ground – with the exception of China and the Middle East – the opportunity to integrate 'sense of place' into new additional terminals and airport refurbishment programmes is great.

Dane County Regional Airport in Madison, Wisconsin is going through a $52,000,000 concourse and terminal expansion programme, which started back in 1998 with the appointment of Architectural Alliance to develop a 20-year masterplan. Architectural Alliance has a special Aviation Studio which has provided solutions for more than 36 airports across America in all aspects of planning and architecture. Their work is in essence a multi-phased exercise for the airport. The design approach chosen was to implement a 'sense of place' ethos based on the region. Inspiration was to come from such elements as local architecture, native landscapes and place-specific connections. What was also crucial to the design application was to create a feel that was very much local rather than what could be described as Middle American. To this end the architectural style was based on an adaptation of the Prairie School ethos. This most interesting of architectural design movements existed from the 1890s until c 1920 and embodied the search for a uniquely American expression for building, echoing the vast horizontal

ABOVE The airport entrance to Dane County showing the full extent of the architectures "sense of place" heritage.

planes of the surrounding Midwestern landscape. Regional materials showcasing local craftspeople were common throughout each building and clearly indicate an affinity with the British Arts and Crafts movement. Wisconsin's favourite son Frank Lloyd Wright – whose estate Taliesin is only 56 kilometres from the project site – figured prominently in this movement, connecting the horizontality of his architecture with the long lines of the common forms of transportation.

The prerequisite for the general contractor at Dane County Regional Airport also followed the 'sense of place' theme in that whoever was appointed had to be located within 60 miles (97 kilometres) of the project site. This may seem to be an excessive restriction but what it achieved was the employment of local craftsmen, thereby aiding the local economy. Project specifications also stipulated that designated materials either extracted or manufactured had also to come from a given radius of the site. For practical purposes 500 miles (805 kilometres) was the limit.

The airport – which is owned by Dane County but, surprisingly, is financially independent in that

ABOVE Interior of the Art Court facing west. The window has a Brazilian granite bench that runs the length of the glass wall. The light coves above illuminate both the ceiling and the Prairie style inspired window at nightfall.

RIGHT The interior of the Art Court complete with display counters exhibiting local art. This is situated in the main ticketing hall which is located between the main entrance doors. Floor is constructed of porcelain tile and the columns have a brick and granite base complete with hand-made tiles cut into them.

LEFT A door detail showing the combination of frosted glass with Art Deco inspired detailing.

BELOW A corner image of the airport building with it's deco inspired construction.

ABOVE The Dane County Regional Airport entrance at night with the vast glass wall illuminated.

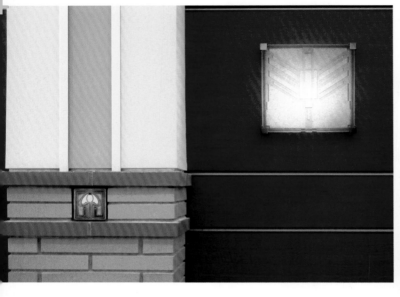

LEFT Ambient light provided by boxed surface lights set into the walls.

RIGHT A gate podium showing the metal detailing that combines both decoration as well as protection in this heavy footfall area, quite a visual treat while you wait for your ticket to be clipped!

it requires no subsidy from the taxpayer – put in place several surveys and focus groups to determine what visitors thought of the existing structure. 'Unrememberable' and 'lacking in distinction' was the general consensus of opinion. And as Madison's own economy is growing faster than the national average, demands on the airport both in terms of air traffic requirements and building multiplied. It is the State capital with a population of nearly a quarter of a million people. It also has a burgeoning business community encompassing bio-tech and other high-tech enterprises as well as a State University.

Even the most cursory of glances at the exterior reveals that inspiration came from Frank Lloyd Wright. Architectural lines are either flat or vertical, emblematic of this important movement. The colour palette chosen by the architects is also crucial to their theme in that it draws its base

from the hues of the local bluffs and foliage. The existing terminal building complements the colour palette as it too had been constructed using very earthy tones.

It is in the interior that one really sees the reality of 'sense of place' and not a single area has been spared the treatment. Ticket desks are constructed with a mixture of stainless steel and cherry wood detailing. A conference facility dedicated to Robert B Skuldt echoes the desks with cherry-coloured walls and etched glass. The project's architects also retained for the airport regional artists and craftsmen who would add their own energies. This can be seen in the retail and refreshment areas, which benefit from having high ceilings. Here there are a variety of illuminated agricultural-inspired patterns, together with images of various local notables that are part of Dane County's history. The use of local artists may

ABOVE This is Dane County Airport's main entrance area where the 'meeters and greeters' ascend the escalator to the security area.

ABOVE The 'meeters and greeters' lounge complete with a gas fired fireplace in brick and granite. The backdrop is a restored 1930s mural depicting what the airport looked like then. It was made in the Depression when the government of the day used to support artists in recording local scenes and events.

LEFT An exterior shot of the south-west corner. The tall glass and steel construction beyond is the ticketing hall with canopies over the entrance.

seem obvious for a 'sense of place' design, but it can be fraught with danger – after all, 'local' does not necessarily go hand-in-hand with 'excellent' and could so very easily spell creative disaster. Fortunately the art pieces give an added value to the environment and some of them do not come in small sizes! A 5-metre by 5-metre granite, quartzite and porcelain artwork executed by John Rieben, Art Professor at University of Wisconsin-Madison, is set into the floor.

Like all new builds in today's global construction world, sustainability was also critical to the design. Outside the terminal building are seating areas designed in a rustic manner with gazebos, wooden benches and brick patios complete with native plants and grasses. Recycling was a big contributor to the construction effort, as part of

the build programme, as was the gathering, sorting and recycling of old building materials and components that would find their way back into the new structure. The percentage is phenomenal – 97 per cent of construction site waste was recycled. The whole project – and there are still certain elements to be built – follows clear 'sense of place' thinking: a recognisably local overall architectural style, and the integration of simple architectural expression into the natural landscape. With masters from Henry Hobson Richardson to the great Frank Lloyd Wright, it is no wonder that Dane County Regional Airport in America's Midwest had such a fabulous array of inspiration for its 'sense of place' architectural style. When it is all finished it has the possibility of becoming an iconic airport for this new genre of design.

RIGHT Natural light was an important part of the interior design of the airport Terminal building.

BELOW The plane is a reproduction of a 1930's Corben Super Ace. The ceiling has acoustic tiles with aluminium accent lighting. Daylight floods in from the first floor windows at the end of the main ticket hall.

ARCHITECTURAL ENHANCEMENT

CASE STUDY: WASHINGTON NATIONAL AIRPORT NORTH TERMINAL, USA

Architect: Cesar Pelli & Associates, USA

Every now and then, along comes a gem: something that is so different and awe-inspiring that it warrants a further and detailed look. For this to happen in airport design, it helps to have an iconic passenger terminal complex as a backdrop, combined with an equally iconic architect – such as Cesar Pelli. The Architectural Enhancement Program (AEP) which has transformed the North Terminal at Washington National Airport marks the highly successful integration of art and architecture – for it is indeed 'integration', rather than mere 'application'. It is not a case of art being applied to a surface like a stamp to an envelope – a more common approach in public building. Instead, this is the full-blown holistic embodiment of the two but in the detail of the building itself.

The North Terminal is located between the South Terminal (built in 1941) and the hangars at the north end of the airport and is approximately 93,000 square metres in area. It has 35 gates and is designed to handle 16 million passengers per year. Like the historic South Terminal, all the financial elements of an airport have been placed firmly on landside, helping to create a vast expanse of glass through which to see Washington's federal buildings beyond. The North Terminal is made up of three levels with ticket counters and departures located on the upper level, the main concourse being on the middle level. This concourse is the

terminal's principal thoroughfare; it is here where one gets a true sense of Pelli's creative thrust.

The AEP involves 30 specially commissioned works of art which have been integrated into the architecture of the North Terminal. In fact it is not just 'art', for that is too simple a word for what has been created. It is the combination of an architect's vision with artistic imagination, artworks and the actual building form, artists and the very necessary artisan input and artwork . What sets this 'art in the environment' programme apart from others is that each specific location, size of artwork and material choice for the artists was decided upon after Pelli had produced a conceptual design for the building. This allowed the works of art to be placed and integrated in the most beneficial manner for both terminal and artwork. This type of marriage between artists and architect to this extent is nothing new; there are many such illuminating examples, the Rockefeller Center in New York and the Los Angeles Central Library being just two successful pre-Second World War examples. As Pelli explains:

> The idea of having artists work in architecture was very much alive through the 1930s up until the Second World War. After that, there were changes in the self-conceptions of both artists and architects that made it very difficult to have paintings and

ABOVE The main concourse of the Terminal building.

sculpture integrated with the buildings. This hiatus was created by an extreme glorification of the individual ego and individual freedom that came with post-Second World War Modernism. Most architects, like most painters and sculptors, are trained in their schools, in their friendships, and in their professional cultures, to consider themselves as the only creators and to believe that no-one else should come to interfere in their creations. I think that there is an isolation between architects and artists that is a form of impoverishment for

both sides. At best, we have gotten pieces of sculpture placed in front of buildings as independent elements working in counterpoint with the building. I can think of many that are very handsome, but they are not part of the architecture.

One can easily see a hint of sadness in Pelli's comment, but it is also possibly not the whole story. What about the client? All parties involved in a cultural endeavour have to be sympathetic to the common aim. For it wasn't just Pelli and the artists, it was also the tremendous foresight of the airport's management that provided the backdrop

ABOVE Washington National Airport, North Terminal. A photograph of the exterior roof shape and windows to the Terminal.

RIGHT This image shows the 2Art Glass" panelling in the main Terminal window.

for this to work. Dan Feil, Design Project Manager for the Metropolitan Washington Airports Authority, was its lynchpin – the person in tune with the architect's desire and the person who wholeheartedly embraced this form of art integration.

There were of course several creative and practical problems to solve in the partnership of art and artisan. Each work of art had, with only two exceptions, to be integrated into the building's surface material. It also meant that by its very nature the majority of the 30 artists would be working in a material alien to their normal genre of work. There would be metal, porcelain, mosaic tiles for floor medallions and glass for the window friezes. Then there is artwork scale to take on board: enlarging a painting from half size to full size not only affects colour but can also alter the momentum of the work itself. Considerable co-operation was needed between the artists and the artisans in order to best achieve what both could give to the work – 'both' being the operative word. In reality the transformation process simply added a richness to the work of art; this is particularly prevalent in the 10 large floor medallions and the 110 glass frieze panels. It could have been a very arduous creative process; fortunately

for the muralists and sculptors they were able to execute their work single-handedly.

Who, then, are the artists and what did they create? As the city is Washington and, some would say, 'the cultural heart of America' it is only fitting that the list of artists involved reads like a *Who's Who* of the very best American contemporary art: Caio Fonseca, Wayne Edson Bryan, Cary Smith, Vincent Longo, Edith Kuhnle, Nancy Graves, Sol LeWitt, Frank Stella and Richard Anuszkiewicz, to name but a few. They are all at the very top of their craft and stature.

The locations for each of the artworks were identified as 'art sites' and all are situated in the interior of the terminal. For the balustrade of the upper concourse 10 artists were commissioned to produce six panels each. Three of each artist's panels face inward, visible from the upper level, and three are directed for viewing from the lower concourse. Ten artists' works were the colossal 5.5-metre-diameter medallions set into the black, red, yellow and grey geometrically patterned terrazzo floor on the lower concourse. For the window walls facing the runways and aircraft there are etched friezes, each comprising 55 panels measuring 0.6 by 2.4 metres. These can be seen equally well

RIGHT Washington National Airport, North Terminal. This image shows Michele Oka Doner's work *Flight*, a medallion made out of terrazzo marble and cast bronze, measuring 5.5 metres in diameter.

LEFT Washington National Airport, North Terminal. The contribution of Frank Stella, one of the great American artists, to the Architectural Enhancement Program is a 5.5-metre-diameter medallion called *Hooloomooloo*, made of marble and glass.

from both concourse levels. The rest of the 'art sites' comprise four unique locations that still work within the building as the programme required. Robert Vickery's mural is set in a stainless steel wall that encloses a food and drink area within the terminal. All the artworks are on a scale not normally either seen by the public or executed by the artists: the 2.4- by 7.3-metre murals are a good example.

One commentator, John Pastier, has stated that 'the North Terminal is a 1,600 foot long Noah's Ark of contemporary artists'. In that case the 'two by two' here are the artist and artisan. Washington National Airport was first designed 60 years ago when any form of travel was an elite activity, just for the well heeled. What Pelli has achieved is to offer art in a very pluralist mode, something for everyone to engage with. It is not an art gallery, it is an airport environment built with art, and passengers will have an almost subliminal appreciation of the art there. It is powerful and above all it is the most marvellous 'enhancement' the travelling public could experience.

ABOVE Washington National Airport, North Terminal. Here the upper-floor balustrade is a work of art by Siah Armajani. It is constructed out of steel, cast bronze and copper and is 44 metres in length.

RIGHT Here we can see just how high and naturally bright the Terminal building is.

SEATING DESIGN

CASE STUDY: HELSINKI-VANTAA AIRPORT, FINLAND AND GUANGZHOU BAIYUN INTERNATIONAL AIRPORT, CHINA

Designer: Rodney Kinsman, OMK Design, London, UK

If you thought airport chairs were for sitting on, think again! They are for standing on, supporting luggage, common receptacles for food and beverage leftovers, and if you are in some airports in the world that have a problem with unwanted guests, an object on which to vent your hatred. Sitting? You have got to be joking – that is, of course, unless you are the airport operator, because they take great pride in their furniture selection.

The evolution of airport seating, both in design and production, has mirrored the enthusiasm for temple-like airport structures – after all, one cannot have a cheap-looking chair in a Pelli-, Piano- or Rogers-designed airport terminal. It just would not do at all. Chair design has to a certain extent tracked the preferences of people using the airport, and it is more relevant now than when, in the aftermath of the Second World War, international passengers enjoyed the comforts of a leather armchair, early-movie-style, in the huts that made up the then aerodrome. These chairs fitted the passenger profile – well off and 'international', the chairs could have come straight out of their drawing rooms. Design first entered the airport marketplace at Chicago's O'Hare Airport with the adoption of a Charles Eames specially designed chair. Surprisingly these chairs can still be seen today despite their inability to stand up to the

rigours of today's airport environment. The chair is essentially a stretched deck chair but in leather. This was the 1950s.

One of the most important chairs to describe the evolution to what we see and use today is the Conran 'Terminus' chair, designed for British Airways in the 1960s. It was essentially a low-tech bench-style seat, rather over-generous in size. The idea was that you could cram the passengers on because it did not have any arms. It might seem good for its time but essentially it had too big a footprint.

A turning point in airport chair design came with the introduction of more sophisticated fire regulations which not only covered the building shell but also the contents. OMK Design, a London-based commercial furniture design business, was approached by Gatwick Airport in the 1980s to design a chair that conformed to the regulations. As a result the 'Transit' seat was born and installed in the North Terminal. The design was simple and executed in steel to what was then a very demanding brief, as the maintenance factor was critical to the airport operator. Once again the design was low-tech and simple, a tubular steel frame complete with pressed steel panels. For OMK Design as a company, this was the start of a fascination with the airport world and

ABOVE Guangzhou Baiyun International Airport. This image clearly emphasises how the 'Trax' system is constructed. The metal frame is made of cast aluminium which is fixed to a triangular sub-frame. Note the clearance height from the floor, which assists floor cleaning and visibility for security purposes.

RIGHT 'Trax' seating system. The original sketch by the designer Rodney Kinsman showing just how the construction was formulated: a series of components individually costed and then added to a variety of bases.

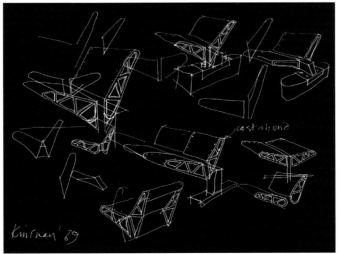

ABOVE Guangzhou Baiyun International Airport. Seating at Departure Gate D. Here the seating is in green which is the gate colour and is part of the way-finding scheme at the airport.

designing for it, leading them to use manufacturing processes that are far removed from traditional chair-making.

Chair design is inevitably tied to the needs of the individual, but in the case of airport seating it is also tied to what type of passenger you are, be it first class, business class or charter. There can be a chair for any passenger level and it is worth noting that these levels can change as an airport's destination and carrier traffic changes. For the airport, let alone the chair designer and manufacturer, the scenario can be an ever-changing one.

OMK Design's 'Trax' system was originally developed as a low-cost seating solution for the UK's British Rail network. Here the system had to embrace both the mass end of the market together with passengers who were travelling first class. 'Trax' is a kit of parts with interchangeable panels that can encompass hard and soft surfaces.

This flexibility allows easy maintenance as the seating rows cannot be removed. Rodney Kinsman comments: 'Chairs are seen as a statement in airports but as a product it has to be flexible. It cannot break down and has to be a visually timeless product – nothing to do with fashion – and must stay in use for over 25 years.'

The airport chair marketplace is a highly competitive one with maybe 30 to 40 major manufacturers and a market that is driven by the manufacturer with technology. The inevitable 'copying' that takes place demonstrates the size of the market, despite having a potentially negative effect on companies such as OMK Design.

OMK Design's work for Helsinki-Vantaa Airport is a good example of how the market works. It is essentially a partnership: here Helsinki required a high-level product that not only looked good but was also indestructible. The answer was for OMK

ABOVE LEFT Guangzhou Baiyun International
Airport. The 'Trax' system in a multiple configuration
format based on a two-chair, three-chair and four-chair
configuration.

ABOVE RIGHT Guangzhou Baiyun International
Airport. 'Trax' seating from the outside.

BELOW Guangzhou Baiyun International Airport. A
bird's-eye view showing how the seating system can
be joined together with a table in-between.

ABOVE Guangzhou Baiyun International Airport. The 'Trax' system, designed originally back in 1989 by Rodney Kinsman and developed since then by his company OMK. Consisting of a steel perforated seat and back with leather upholstery, here it is in a three-seat configuration, complete with integral table.

Design to cover a 'Trax' frame in coach hide. Helsinki loved it, but also required an even higher-grade product for a certain passenger profile, so the seat was softened and a high back and footrest were added.

Guangzhou Baiyun International Airport's seating project amply demonstrates that the airport chair business is very much a global one and with it come problems that need to be addressed. The total seating requirement was 14,000 – a colossal number when a normal contract is 2,000–3,000. Timescale from start to finish was only four months, and that included a one-month transportation time at sea. The contract with OMK Design was full of penalties, particularly regarding questions of time and installation. Their choice was the 'Trax' system fitted with four different pastel-shade leather seats.

Design is not all about practical and aesthetic solutions: there are cultural differences that in some parts of the globe have to be taken on board. The common one is that in some countries women cannot sit next to men, as in Istanbul Atatürk Airport – there has to be a perceived gap, which can be a half a table size. This allows for a

chair company to build up a system that can be a kit of parts, which for today's airport and its seating requirements is essential. It promotes not only chairs for each specific passenger market but also an overall look of harmony.

Wear and tear, and the prevention of it, is a critical issue. Here OMK Design have developed a moulded polyurethane seat that can even be slashed with a knife. The cut is still there but it visually heals. It is ongoing development like this that is important to the marketplace.

How, then, do companies such as OMK Design get business? It sounds dangerous to an outsider – the production of a prototype with no design fees charged. Ouch! What is essential is that the size of the project needs to be significant and therefore commercially viable. A touch of corporate confidence in what you produce might not be bad either! It is in the manufacturing process that profits are made or lost. Many airport chair companies operate a holistic approach involving both design and production. For OMK Design this has never been the route; in fact they went outside of the chair manufacturing industry completely – the car industry was to provide not only

ABOVE Guangzhou Baiyun International Airport. The 'Trax' system at a Guangzhou Airport departure gate.

effective production but also the latest technological solutions both in materials and in production methods. Car component companies manufacture tens of thousands of components to a very high standard, and OMK have used this as their base. It is high volume, ultra-competitive and leads to a whole different range of technical expertise. It is a most unusual approach but one in which there are no fixed overheads, no downtime, and you only pay for what you produce and need. As Kinsman states, 'It is not a cottage industry, if you treat it as such then you will die.'

Kinsman's company amply demonstrates both excellent airport chair design and innovative production methods. If only the passengers could just sit in the chairs rather than be intent on destroying them!

ABOVE Helsinki-Vantaa Airport. The 'Trax' system here has been advanced by the application of leather for the passengers. The addition of both a foot- and a headrest demonstrates the versatility of the design.

LEFT Guangzhou Baiyun International Airport. The 'Trax' system both airside and landside, placed on a diagonal line.

BELOW Istanbul Atatürk Airport. Here the 'Trax' seating has full upholstery for passenger comfort complete with the critical space needed between the seats.

always been a large problem. The client needs to understand that good lighting design provides a significant visual return for the investment and can transform a terminal from 'ordinary' to 'magnificent'. From this aspect alone there is a very great commercial benefit for the airport operator. Light brightens people's lives! It is therefore not surprising that lighting designers do not speak in terms of lux levels or lighting equipment, but rather about what is appropriate for the many different types of passengers who use an airport, from tourists to businesspeople to nervous flyers. It is about how people feel, and how lighting can affect this in a positive way.

This was at the very heart of Speirs and Major Associates' work on the Madrid Barajas International Airport in Spain. Based in Edinburgh, Scotland, Speirs and Major Associates are a company world-renowned for producing innovative

lighting design solutions, including those for the 'Gherkin', Norman Foster's London headquarters for Swiss Re. Their work for Madrid was in collaboration with the two terminal architects Richard Rogers Partnership of London and Estudio Lamela of Madrid. Here the issues were to do with enhancing the passenger experience by sympathetically expressing the architecture in a cost-effective manner. It was a collaboration of the closest kind, with all concerned wanting to create a very special project. To quote the designer Jonathan Speirs: 'Nothing appeared to be too difficult if it benefited the project … not all projects run this way!'

The work itself evolved with a series of intense and long workshops where concepts and details were thrashed out over a relatively short period. It also helped having a client who was particularly supportive of the lighting philosophy and creative

ABOVE The circular rooflighting system by Speirs and Major together with the colour-coded signage for each of the three terminals.

thinking that went into the solutions. The main area lighting was achieved by a mirror reflector system located at the translucent rooflight screens, with the luminaires placed in a custom-designed frame suspended below the rooflights. Madrid Barajas International Airport's new terminal has an extraordinary bamboo roof (see the next Case Study in this book, focusing on its ceiling) that was actually an asset to the lighting solution; it had a soft way of taking light. The roof was lit by means of pre-directed spill light but this was localised to ensure the roof structure maintained its dynamic rhythm. The lower levels had an expressive lighting system for the ceiling that was referred to during the design process as the 'woks' and allowed large areas of the concrete soffits to remain exposed. These 'woks' had a downlight component with a reflector ring to redirect some of this light back up onto the dishes.

This was a fast-track project that dictated a shorthand method of working and, as already mentioned, a close working relationship was required from the outset. Simon Smithson from Richard Rogers Partnership was the key person who ensured that both natural light and artificial light worked not only together but also to the building's advantage. The natural lighting design was the responsibility of Arup Associates with local engineers Biosca & Botey, and was in itself a tremendous success. It is essential in any building, especially a commercial one, that a balance is achieved between natural and artificial light. For airports that operate on a 24/7 basis this is of paramount importance for all the reasons given. Madrid Barajas International Airport's new terminal is a very good example of what can be achieved when people do not work in isolation. Perhaps it was the pressure resulting from the limited timescale of the project that helped all the creative protagonists to produce a terminal of outstanding beauty as well as practicality – and one which was awarded the RIBA Stirling Prize 2006.

BELOW The Gate area showing how the Speirs and Major-designed lighting system complements the curved bamboo ceiling installed by Lindner.

CEILING DESIGN

CASE STUDY: MADRID BARAJAS INTERNATIONAL AIRPORT, SPAIN

Architects: Richard Rogers Partnership, London, UK; Estudio Lamela, Madrid, Spain
Supplier: Lindner, Arnstorf, Germany

'Look to the heavens' is an ecclesiastical phrase and one not normally associated with airports. Cathedrals maybe, but certainly not airports. An airport had to have a roof on to keep the travellers dry, and that is as far as the investment and design initiative used to go. If you did raise your eyes, you would and probably still do see row upon row of wrinkly tin ducts and dust-covered supporting structures. Not a pleasant sight at all! To be fair, the passenger was too concerned with finding the check-in desk or departure gate to even think about was going on above. Fast-forward to now and the general public has become only too aware of building design – it is being discussed on television night and day. It is now engrained in the public's psyche, at whatever level.

The general public now do want to be stimulated by what they see. Madrid Barajas International Airport is an exciting building. The creative partnership of Richard Rogers and Estudio Lamela has created a most magnificent new terminal that is rich both in aesthetic qualities and in technological features. This winning design – for there was an open international competition – is not set in stone; built in is the flexibility and versatility to expand the building's envelope for increased passenger requirements in the future. To say that the roof is of key importance to the terminal would be an overstatement, but it is integral to the whole design concept and awesome to

look at. On a practical note it takes an airport terminal roof fit-out to another level.

The first thing that one senses about the airport's recently completed ceiling is the sheer scale of its inspiring wave shape. This was the first challenge to be faced in its design: what material has the flexibility to be able to 'fit' such an undulating structure? There was also another criterion that had to be satisfied, and that was the emphasis on ecological factors for the building. As a result bamboo was chosen because it complied with both of these elements: it is a fast-growing plant and also has the inherent capacity to be shaped. Lindner, the airport fit-out company, was able to fulfil the brief and come up with a bamboo product that could both fit the wave formation of the ceiling and, because it is a public building, meet all the required fire and safety standards.

The density of their bamboo product is commensurate to oak, and as it is a grass it has the ability to bend naturally even when it becomes a more fibrous product. Lindner chose to use bamboo trunks aged four to five years; this was to ensure a specific hardness that was required to make the panels. All the bamboo used came from one plantation in China and was vigorously checked in panel form to ensure that it met all the necessary physical attributes. In all 1,400 kilometres of bamboo panels were produced for the airport's ceiling covering – a total of 280,000 square metres.

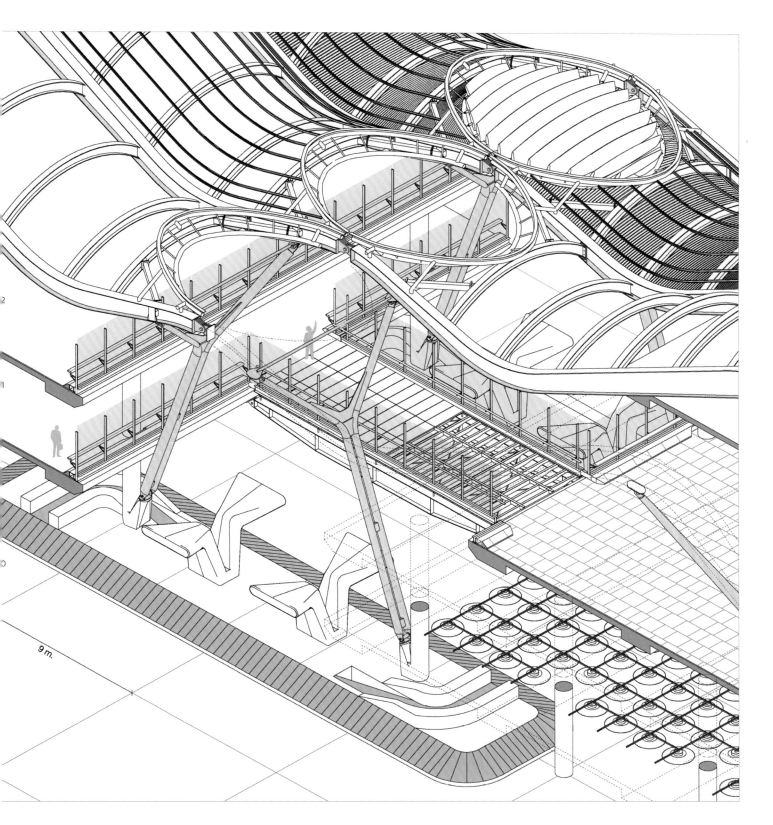

9 m.

ABOVE A see-through graphic of the terminal building at all its levels and applications.

LEFT An exterior image of the curved roof and gate connections to the planes.

BELOW LEFT The colour-coded uprights for each of the three terminals.

BELOW RIGHT The bamboo ceiling is curvaceous in form and is constructed in panels.

Following various unfortunate happenings, safety in airports has been top of any airport operator's list, and so it was at Madrid. How is a bamboo product going to pass stringent tests such as those for fire-resistance? Lindner developed a technique for treating the bamboo, which enabled the material to be impregnated with a special fire protection element so that it was able to meet the MI fire standard. One interesting feature of the ceiling is that not only are the bamboo panels used in all their glory inside, but also on the exterior underneath roof surface, which amounts to approximately 80,000 square metres.

It is not just the ceiling that is a success; the modus operandi of the working relationship between architects and suppliers is also worth noting, as is Lindner's own way of promoting design ideas. Companies such as Lindner were involved very early on, virtually at concept stage. This both helps the tendering process and, when

the go-ahead is given, allows all parties concerned to work more easily in what is often a very short timeframe. This saves both time and cost and is a process that needs to be brought into the airport build arena more often, especially when it is either a terminal extension or a refurbishment programme where both time constraints and the practical elements of the terminal still being in operation are concerned.

Fit-out companies are more and more frequently being asked to resolve questions and put forward design proposals. Lindner provided their ideas as computer-generated 3-D animations. These came from instructions provided on factors such as materials, values for sound absorption and other critical criteria. What this does is to enable a fit-out company to show its creative endeavours in resolving problems, not just a set of bland numbers. The choice can then be made in a more holistic manner and problems resolved a lot earlier.

ABOVE This image shows how the ceiling is constructed at passenger gate level.

RETAIL

The fact of flight remains at the very heart of what an airport is and why passengers go there, but retail runs a very close second. There are those who go to an airport purely to see and experience the global brand phenomena on offer. It is also worth remembering that airports can employ tens of thousands of people who need to shop on any level for sheer practicality. The rise of retail as a major earner for airport operators has been a long and sometimes tortuous path.

As has previously been mentioned, the first flights took off from aerodromes, nothing more than a field and a shack. Retail arrived a lot later but was still only a shop or, worse, a kiosk that sold one of everything and nothing in particular. This was of course an inter-war situation, but it was still going to be a long-haul flight to what we have today. America, that pinnacle of retailing, was the first country to spread its retail wings into airports – but even here it lacked the appeal and sophistication of what was happening in the shopping malls across the USA. It seems strange that for a continent so bound up in retailing and having now some of the largest, most successful retailers in the world, there is still a long way to go in adopting airport retail philosophies. These philosophies, which are now helping to shape the airport retail offer, emanate from Europe.

Fast-forward to today and you find a complex situation that encompasses many different specialists, let alone the retailers themselves. There is also the question of landside versus airside, which represent two totally different shopping venues but in themselves may have exactly the same retail brands in their separate locations. This may appear bizarre, since both locations will also have the same clientele – so what is the difference? The whole process is driven by the mindset of the passenger. Landside can equal stress, as this is pre-security, where all the nitty-gritty of check-in happens. Airside also has various 'local' conundrums as security, boarding pass and passport control can all happen in this area. For the purpose of assessing the different retail scenarios, 'boarding pass' is where the mindset changes.

Airside retailing has grown over the last decade both in space and in levels of retail sophistication. Some of this, particularly in Europe, can be put down to the demise of Duty Free trade. More importantly it is to do with a better understanding of how passengers operate. Airside space as a proportion of the entire retail offer can be as high as 85 per cent, particularly in Europe. In America

ABOVE Berry Bros & Rudd. A wide selection of illuminated display cabinets acting as an attractive and enticing backdrop to the shop.

LEFT Liquor Bar. This promotional bar, used here to promote the Johnnie Walker whisky brand, helps to keep passengers in the 'sales' zone — it even has stools, once again adding to the experience.

it can be as low as 65 per cent. A passenger will always be able to buy a magazine or sun cream from the same retail brand in both airside and landside; but once airside, choice opens up and can be a lot more market-targeted. Luxury goods are an ideal example.

Retailing in airports is important, but where does the process actually start? If it is a proactive airport it could begin in the passenger's home, with awareness not just of what brands are available but also of price guarantees, offers and the like. Amsterdam Schiphol Airport has adopted a pre-airport marketing programme using a variety of above- and below-the-line marketing activities in order to strengthen what is already a very comprehensive retail offer. It is an ongoing message that seeks both to promote and to reaffirm what Schiphol Airport is about commercially.

At the very heart of an airport's commercial success is masterplanning – it is here that an architect or designer can really make a mark, but it is not as simple as a shopping mall. Most commercial masterplanning nowadays happens for airports which are already open and operating at full stretch on all fronts. Airports have to make a financial return and they do have a captive audience for two hours plus. It is not only about the arrangement of shop locations and footfall past these retailers, it can also concern itself with the 'encouragement' of the airlines themselves to free up much-needed space by moving their office function off-site. For a new airport build, provided that the structures architect and the interior architect work together, the process can be an invigorating one. Gatwick North Terminal is an excellent example of the simple expansion of the building envelope coupled with a radical overhaul of retailing space based on the passenger's journey to the gate.

Developing the retail mix has always been critical for airports, and is a field that is still evolving. Airports need the global brands, which are now expected by the customer; but they also need to be a showcase for what is excellent *locally*. Here 'locally' does not mean an extension of the local bazaar! Airports have a golden opportunity to showcase their countries' own brands, which in some cases could be global as well. Sydney Airport is such a place but with a fierce nationalistic pride that sees the Aussie offer mixed in with global retailers, successfully bouncing off each other.

Designing for the airport retail market is not as straightforward as the high street or mall, and nor are the retail practices. Opening hours are long and footfall hopefully continuous but with peaks and troughs. How do you brand a shop when it does not have a front? Then there is the situation of time-critical passenger perception. WH Smith plc have for a long time operated as passenger terminal retailers encompassing coach, rail and flight. The brand has remained strong throughout, helped by the design of the detail and a thorough understanding of the passenger terminal marketplace stretching over a century.

Transforming the retail brand to the airport marketplace is not an easy option, even if you are well known on the high street. Imagine being in charge of a brand born over 400 years ago, iconic in status, but only known to a few. To branch out into the airport sphere would on the face of it seem like financial suicide, but Berry Bros & Rudd, purveyors of wine and spirits to the British royal family, took that leap of faith on the back of advancing technology. Successful brand transference was critical, as was their retailing methodology. It also helped that the airport operator had caseloads of encouragement and support for such a precious British retail institution. You do not have to be 400 years old as a retailer to gain from their experience; it is a showcase example of a well-planned and well-executed retailing step.

Duty Free has always been popular with the travelling public. The European Union's curtailing of it was not! Fortunately in some parts of the globe it is still seen as the cornerstone of airport retailing. Bangkok International Suvarnabhumi Airport's Duty Free is both extensive and meticulously organised. Here there is a difference in that all products on sale are first purchased by the retailing company running the airport's commercial activity and then sold by them. It is an unusual methodology.

BAA plc represents the very zenith of what being an operator of the commercial activities of an airport is. Its transformation from government department through to being one of the largest global companies in this marketplace is an interesting journey. What matters more is its views on 'partnerships' with retailers and others, its methodology for employing architects and designers and its quite radical approach to seeking out new retailing enterprises to bring into the fold. The company's management and strategic thinking are at the very core of its success. For retailers, other commercial operators and the many specialists that are used by the company, this case study represents an insight into the world of commerce in successful airports.

This section of the book is not just about retail; it is concerned with how the passenger is looked after in the very best sense. From home to gate, airport retailing is omnipresent – and success equals cash tills ringing, together with happy passengers.

TOP The entrance to the WH Smith bookshop at Heathrow Terminal 3.

BOTTOM WH Smith, Heathrow Airport Terminal 1. The merchandising units at Gatwick North Terminal airport bookshop are shown here in wood.

AIRPORT BRANDING

CASE STUDY: VENICE MARCO POLO INTERNATIONAL AIRPORT, ITALY

Architect: JHP Design

The word 'branding' has been a cause of delight among graphic design professionals for over 25 years now. There are also derivatives of this such as re-branding and brand-complementation. You name it, and it could be branded. In reality there are some elements of commercial life where branding is perhaps not needed, or has to be used in a very subtle way, and airports fall into this category. The first question that should be asked is: is it a benefit to the user? In this case, the user is the passenger. There are some important elements to travel that passengers not only want to know but can feel very stressed about: time of cab, check-in desk, gate and airline.

Tradition has it that airport branding has always been about either location- or people-driven names – Heathrow Airport in England or Charles de Gaulle Airport in Paris, for example. These two have more recently changed their 'brands' to London Heathrow and CDG. What relevance to today's traveller has a small town or a faded politician? None. Adding a differentiator to an airport's name may gratify those connected with the area but it has to 'perform' and not be seen by passengers as a meaningless add-on.

JHP Design, based in London, had to work with the Marco Polo addition but chose to use it as a subtext to communicate the quality and value of what the Venice airport had to offer the passengers, such as retail and food and beverage. Venice is a

'resort', a holiday destination where people go to observe, learn and, for some, wallow in times past – so there is at least a perception of something that is both unique and special to the visitor. What JHP Design created was a series of graphic designs that could be used to promote quality and value, the essence of what Venetians used to trade in during the Renaissance. Iconography and colour associated with Venice were subtly used on banners promoting price point guarantees. What makes this 'branding' exercise so different is the nature of the language employed: it is almost subliminal to the passenger. A light hand has been used in the selection of the colour palette, which combines Venetian tones found on the buildings with the iconic blue of the lagoon. Imagery of everyday life has been pared back to a minimum. The ubiquitous gondola pole; the often-seen *palazzi* reflected in the Grand Canal – both have been used in a very clever manner, the gondola pole to hold a title together whilst the letters are inverted like a reflection in the water. All these images have been used to promote retail and as a reminder of Venice itself.

JHP Design have answered a very difficult problem successfully in only using icons that are obvious to the passengers around them when they are in Venice. It is a creative process that has been based on a 'less-is-more' principle and for that reason it is a great piece of graphic communication.

ABOVE CLOCKWISE The branding promotes the airport of Venice and its association with water, hence the reflective graphics; a graphic using the iconic imagery of the gondola moorings of Venice; the blue of the lagoon used together with the reflection of Venice's Grand Canal to emphasise the airport's domain; a simple graphic image, but utilising one of the typical colours of Venetian architecture.

RIGHT British Airways/London Heathrow Airport branding. Early printed matter produced in various languages to show what British Airways had to offer at London Heathrow Airport.

RETAIL AND COMMERCIAL MASTERPLANNING

CASE STUDY: GATWICK AIRPORT NORTH TERMINAL, UK

Architect: The Design Solution, London
Operators: BAA plc, UK

If there is one factor above all others that makes for a commercially successful airport then it is effective commercial masterplanning. Get this wrong, or do not do it at all, and financial disaster is imminent.

What is a wonder is that commercial masterplanning, especially for retail, is still not universally accepted as an essential component of new airport design. In short it is only thought about after the airport's envelope has been decided, and that is far too late. It is not solely the fault of the prospective airport operator; they have been blinded to commercial reason by overbearing architects who prefer to focus on aesthetics. This is a continuing tragedy for both operator and passengers alike. In America, shopping mall retailing is among the most sophisticated in the world and yet the airports are light years behind Europe in good retail provision. China, with a long history of world trade but lacking in retail on the home front, has taken on board the need to have a fully integrated commercial masterplan in the proposed building before a brick has been laid. As a consequence passenger terminal architects have been forced into joining up with retail architects as part of a joint team in order to secure the design contract for the airport.

Starting from the bottom up is obviously the ideal, but even in cases of airport reconfiguration or extension due to passenger and carrier growth, there are some key elements that need to be applied to any commercial masterplan.

1. The goal should be to direct all passenger flow past all shops. It is not always possible but it should be the priority.

2. Make sure that retail is clearly visible from key passenger routes.

3. Integrate seating areas, which could be food and beverage facilities, into the masterplan to assist in encouraging passengers to remain amongst the commercial space rather than moving off to gates.

4. If, through site constraints, it is necessary to trade on more than one level, catering should be on the upper level. Passengers are more likely to 'travel' to that area than to retail.

5. Shops should have a variety of depths to the units to enable retailers with different trading formats to retail to their optimum without wasting valuable commercial frontage.

6. In order to hold passengers in retail-led lounges, adequate flight information screens should be planned to keep people informed in the trading area.

In producing a commercial masterplan for an airport there is a lot of logical information that can be applied. When passengers and well-wishers first arrive at the airport, they are in no mood to shop. They want clear signage to direct them to check-in, where they can deal with the formalities

ABOVE This image at ground level clearly demonstrates the new uncluttered retail layout.

RIGHT The last expansion element of the space in the left area at lower level and upper mezzanine. A gentle curve of retail as the passengers walk by.

FAR RIGHT The end result of the lower lounge-level extension of retail space completed in 2001.

TOP LEFT A shop full of 'heritage' Aboriginal products such as boomerangs, textiles and artworks. This style of retail outlet is typical of what can be done at an airport. If executed well it is the last chance a passenger has for purchasing something of the country visited, but it is important to have the right product mix and backdrop for it to succeed. **TOP RIGHT** This image shows how cleverly all brands, both Aussie and International, can come together. Here the colour palette, ceiling material and flooring provide the background so the retail brands shine through.
ABOVE LEFT Boost is an Australian food brand situated in a prime spot within the global brand food court.
ABOVE RIGHT An overall view of the retail walk-through at Terminal 1 Pier B showing a very pale colour palette which in turn emphasises the retail offer.

extension of Piers B and C together with the Departure Hall. Both piers had large atriums for the 'Sydney Experience'. The number of shops went from 75 to 138 situated in a retail 'oasis' within the concourses.

Sydney Airport's retail philosophy is that, and I quote, 'retail offerings need to have considerable merit and deliver a level of uniqueness not only against domestic retail offers but also create a point of difference with other international airport retail'. It is easy to see the Australian competitive spirit in such an all-encompassing philosophy – they will take on all comers in their quest to be the best! Sydney Airport's retail offering ranges from exclusive labels, uniquely Australian brands and an international Duty Free to essentials for the traveller and visitor alike. The airport in their retail growth have also taken into account airport dynamics such as traffic flows, sight lines, adjacencies, dwell times

and time and distance in the overall planning and positioning of the retail offer.

The mix of the local and the global was based on a strategy that gave importance and credibility to the local offer within the retail mix as a whole. The Australian retailers include RM Williams, Purely Australian, Beach Culture, The Rainbow Serpent, Oroton, Purely Merino and Done Art & Design. All these stores have been sited in strategic locations amongst the other international brands, thereby ensuring that the passengers are exposed to a comprehensive range of both international and local retail.

What Sydney Airport has fully recognised is that their commercial offer is not set in stone: it is always evolving and developing. Income growth since the Olympics has exceeded passenger growth, and that in 2005 stood at 9.4 million passengers compared with 7.7 million in 1999 – so

Purely, an Australian retail brand that uses the famous 'outback' style. The national sporting colours reinforce the brand image, as does the 'sun and blue sky' graphic. There is a section dedicated to kids' merchandise, and even the product ticketing emphasises the 100 per cent Aussie pedigree. A proud store indeed!

Beach Culture, an Australian retail offer strictly for the young. In many people's minds, Australia is synonymous with beaches; this shop plays on that subconscious link very successfully in its style of retailing and merchandise selection.

Done Store, an Aussie store at its best! Done Art & Design, a well-known Australian store using Aussie artwork and graphic images that reinforce the 'home-brand' style with confidence.

LEFT A truly global brand offer in 'home entertainment'. This could be England, France or Norway, it just happens to be Australia – but still the bright red is used, as are the typical Virgin merchandising units.

the shareholders must be happy. It is an ongoing situation as the airport has launched a major redevelopment plan called 'Project STAR' – State of The Art Renewal. The airport business is a competitive one per se and in order to keep theirs at the top they have accepted the challenge of the government-owned airports such as Singapore's Changi, Dubai, Beijing and Hong Kong. The proposed upgrade is a most significant one, with a major retail development of Terminal 2, which is one of two terminals that handle the large volume of domestic traffic. It will provide a 1,300-square-metre expansion of the terminal and a repositioning of the escalators so that all the departing passengers are exposed to a critical mass of retail and food offerings before moving on to the departure piers. Overall there will be a 50 per cent increase in trading space, taking the total area up to 5,000 square metres.

The Project STAR programme was delivered in stages with the Food Court opened in March 2006 and the rest following over a remarkably short timespan of only 12 months. It is a most significant development programme that will continue to improve the retail mix with elements such as new specialist retail tenancies, but also for Terminal 1 an expansion that takes in the new generation of aircraft with the arrival of the Singapore Airlines A380.

The modernisation process has not only been about 'expansion' and 'strategy': exciting design concepts and cluster offerings are helping to add to the shopping experience. It was good at the start of the century and through innovation and creativity seems to improve on an ongoing basis. Rather like their sports teams!

LEFT Global perfume brands located on the way to "Gates" complete with a "Local"discount offer attached.

OVERLEAF A virtual "multi" food offer located all in one area for passenger convenience and choice.

AIRPORT SHOP DESIGN AND RETAIL PRACTICES
CASE STUDY: WH SMITH PLC, UK

TOP The bold use of the WHSmith logo in 3D fashion.

RIGHT WH Smith plc branding. The recently revamped WHSmith logo.

If you are a well-known international brand with a significant position on the high street, then you might assume that transferring to an airport would be a simple design procedure. It is not; everything apart from the product is different, and even here there may be subtle range differences. Space is a very large consideration, as is the actual shape of that space. There is also, of course, the fact that opening hours are somewhat longer, so staffing requirements are different.

What about the shopper? He or she is in a different mindset from the high street. Shoppers can be either product- or time-focused, and possibly even both. Time, as one can imagine, is a major consideration in an airport – and even here there are differences. Are you landside or in the more relaxed atmosphere of airside? As one can see, there are very fundamental differences to be taken into account both from a shop design angle and of with regard to the actual retail practices that go into making a successful airport store.

WH Smith plc is one of the UK's leading retail brands, steeped in history and the first to engage in passenger terminal retailing. For it is not only in airports that they have a retail presence, but also in rail terminals, and as such they can transfer tried and tested methods and design between the two.

The first WH Smith airport store opened at Heston Aerodrome in 1934, quickly followed by several others at other aerodromes during that year. Heathrow had its first store in 1940. One should take on board the word 'aerodrome' for that is what they were at that time – not 'airports'. It was quite literally a tent or prefabricated hut in the middle of a field, but passenger terminal retailing had been born. From these beginnings WH Smith now has 69 outlets at 22 airports, which are in turn managed in clusters based on the airport terminals. As one can see, some airports have more than one or two stores – this will depend on the airside and landside facilities and terminal space available.

What WH Smith have been able to do is to develop and evolve a 'design standard' that applies to both their rail and airport stores. This is substantially different from their high street design and the differences are mainly due to the tailoring of the product offering. The design philosophy operates from several key points, the first being the size and shape of the space available. After this comes the anticipated footfall which, apart from any other design ethos, is directly related to the number of tills and their subsequent positioning. It now becomes a passenger analysis programme detailing customer types: whether they are travelling for leisure or business; the behaviour of long- or short-haul passengers; and whether they are arriving or departing the airport. Lastly come the passenger flow and the location of the store in the terminal.

ABOVE The entrance to the WH Smith bookshop at Heathrow Terminal 1.

ABOVE RIGHT Corporate use of space for product and sales promotion, so important in airport book purchasing.

There are of course core design elements such as flooring, lighting and finishes, but even here there may be design stipulations by the various airport landlords. For WH Smith their own 'design standard' has changed and evolved over the last two years based on the development work carried out at King's Cross railway station in London. Much of this was in response to their customers' own requirements. These changes have resulted in brighter stores, simpler layouts and easier navigation. All this is about the customer being time-conscious. From this has come the use of light boxes to signpost categories and products rather than the previous use of words on walls. Product display has also changed: it is no longer generic but designed for the specific products that are to be carried, a significant extra investment but one in which both clarity and effective merchandising will ensure a healthy return on capital.

WH Smith's greatest challenge has been that there is no such thing as a typical travel shop. The unique configuration of each shop has a huge impact on the design. Narrow shop fronts, for example, allow less space to inform their customers of any promotional offers and activity that is going on in-store – a significant negative element when compared with the high street or shopping mall. The company's own research indicates that every second counts, which has driven the design of outlets so that customers can navigate the store quickly, select products easily and

pay swiftly. In any passenger terminal, getting the customers through the tills is one of the biggest challenges, due in part to the enormous peaks and troughs in numbers entering the store on both a daily and a seasonal basis.

If there is one thing in retail that contributes to profit, this is effective merchandising – and in passenger terminals it is paramount. When it comes to merchandising for travel shops, it is significantly different from the high street or shopping mall. One critical element is that by their very nature travel shops have smaller shop floors, so it is not possible to have the depth of product range found in a normal store. For WH Smith in the UK its customers know it for its core products – books and magazines that are at the very heart of its retail offer. On top of this for its 'travel' stores are drinks, confectionery and in some cases pre-packed sandwiches and snacks. Some branches, again dependent on the availability of space, will provide 'convenient offerings' of other ranges found in their high street stores such as stationery and cards. With the exception of books and magazines, the staple diet of any traveller, their 'travel' shops also carry ranges that you would not expect to see on the high street such as travel accessories and health and beauty products. Merchandising all these product ranges on a 24/7 basis requires a concerted effort to keep stands full and 'refreshed'. It is also expected by the travelling public who will assume that they can buy their daily newspaper any time from 5 am to 11 pm!

ABOVE WH Smith, Heathrow Airport Terminal 1.
The traditional open-front shop, so necessary for
passengers who 'grab and go'.

ABOVE Here we see a corner store opening to good effect.

Paying for anything can be an absolute nightmare at airports – there is always somebody walking straight to the front! Two years ago and only in their larger outlets WH Smith installed queue systems to make the process of paying a more fair and orderly one. This is for WH Smith an ongoing scheme, which includes them now researching a system where customers will be informed how long they are likely to have to queue, and the installation of self-service tills.

Another element that aids not only the customer but also the in-store staff is the design and development of high-volume fixtures for the large airport stores for product ranges such as magazines, and deep and high drink chillers. This type of airport retail progress has also gone hand-in-hand with product development, as they have recently introduced a specialist books format designed to offer an extended range of books in an environment that facilitates browsing. The first of this store format opened in 2006 in Gatwick North Terminal, UK.

As with all retailing there comes a time when a store re-fit is crucial. Here there appears to be a natural time for such work as stores are managed on a contract period and the re-fit work is carried out in line with the contract. There are of course times when this work is more difficult: the summer, for instance, when footfall is at its highest. Unlike the high street, airports are highly regulated for safety and security reasons, so this aspect also has to be taken into consideration when a re-fit is planned.

Airport retail is retail at it most challenging, especially when it comes to design. It requires both science and technological innovation for product display, promotional activity and store planning. Experts in all these fields are necessary for retailers like WH Smith to continue to evolve and to improve the shopping experience. It is not about 'decorating' and making things 'pretty' – it is hard-core design, pragmatic in its approach and successful in its outcome. WH Smith can be said to be 'old hands' but a lot can be learnt from experience and this company is not resting on its previous laurels.

ABOVE WH Smith, Gatwick Airport North Terminal. This image shows how WH Smith subdivide the bookstore at Gatwick North Terminal. This is the history section.

BELOW WH Smith, Gatwick Airport North Terminal. Here WH Smith have used subtext to advertise the store's concept and product offer.

TRANSFERRING THE BRAND

CASE STUDY: BERRY BROS & RUDD, HEATHROW AIRPORT TERMINAL 3, UK

Designer: Fitch, London, UK

Retailing in airports is not a hit-or-miss operation. Airport operators, be they organisations such as BAA plc or a government authority, have both guidelines and statistical information that assist a retail company in deciding if airports are for them – and when they are, what location, size and retail method they will need. This makes good commercial sense and helps to make the trading transition a little easier because, as we have already seen, a high street store operates differently from an airport outlet. Transferring the brand so that it does not lose its own qualities is at the very heart of successful airport retailing. For global brands with hundreds of shops worldwide it is not necessarily an easy affair, but imagine if you were a single specialist shop in the UK – opening retail outlet number two could be daunting. On top of this, imagine if the original shop opened for 'trade' over 300 years ago. Establishing the second store, and one in an airport retailing environment at that, seems like an impossible task.

Berry Bros & Rudd (BBR) opened their now iconic shop in 1698 at 3 St James's Street, London. It is Britain's oldest wine and spirit merchant and is still run by members of both the Berry and Rudd families. The brand is steeped in the finest traditions, even if some might appear odd. The weighing of customers on the giant coffee scales has

included Lord Byron the poet, William Pitt the gentleman Prime Minister, and the Aga Khan. As you would expect, it has supplied the British royal family since King George III and currently holds two Royal Warrants, for HM The Queen and HRH The Prince of Wales. Transferring the brand has never been more complex, or the challenge more exciting. The traditional interior of the St James's shop is almost exclusively mahogany – and old! Imagine having to fast-forward to MDF, industrially manufactured glass and a coloured interior, all now part of the airport stores.

BBR's introduction to airport retailing came in the early 1990s when BAA, the operator of Heathrow Airport, wanted to open 'the most luxurious shopping area in the world' and approached BBR with a view to being part of this retail experience. The Chairman, Simon Berry, commented at the time that 'this was a unique way of exposing our brand to the world'. BBR opened in 1994 at Terminal 3 in 120 square metres of space with a design reminiscent of an Edwardian library, a kind of physical manifestation of the brand. The space was large and for the first six months it really was about exposing BBR to the world rather than hard and fast sales. The staff, as in 3 St James's, were highly trained but there was a sense that the environment was a little precious and the product

RIGHT The store at Heathrow Airport Terminal 3 with the 'Wine Collection' display unit.

LEFT A close-up view of the very beautiful 'Wine Collection' unit, showing a wide variety of vintage wines.

DUTY FREE

CASE STUDY: BANGKOK INTERNATIONAL SUVARNABHUMI AIRPORT, THAILAND

Operator: King Power
Airport Architect: Murphy/Jahn, Chicago, USA
Retail Architects & Designers: The Design Solution, London, UK; Woodhead International, Sydney, Australia

Suvarnabhumi Airport opened to huge acclaim in August 2006 after several years in the planning and construction phase. Part of the construction process was a reconfiguring of the airport interior prior to its opening. This work involved the removal of part of a 120-metre-long moving walkway, reducing it to just 75 metres, raising of floor levels in the central concourse and other major changes. All of this was in the name of retail, and in particular Duty Free retailing.

This would not have happened were it not for the commercial aptitude of King Power, who were awarded a 10-year contract to run all the commercial activities at the airport, and Airports of Thailand, the airport authority. These decisions were not for the faint-hearted but King Power, working with the design teams of The Design Solution and Woodhead International, understood the need for innovative thinking in producing an interior masterplan that would take Duty Free retailing into the future. Out would go the traditional 'pack it high, sell it cheap' routine so long accepted as part of Duty Free, and in would come product zones providing an enhanced experience for the shopper. King Power's vision did not just stop at the airport but also encompassed an off-site Duty Free complex located in downtown Bangkok.

King Power have a 30-year lease on a five-hectare site granted to the company by the Thai royal family's property department and situated next to the new airport train terminal in the city. The complex is large with 12,000 square metres of retail space, King Power's own new office, a 400-room hotel, restaurants and entertainment facilities. The style of the building's interior is unmistakably Thai. This is done for a very sound commercial reason as at ground-floor level the space is used to showcase Thai handicrafts, an idea developed by King Power with the help of the Department of Export Promotion. The retail mix for the three levels is quite staggering, and while to a certain extent it will mirror the offer at the airport, it will also have a range of concept stores unique to downtown. Retail planning has provided for a walk-through Duty Free area that includes 1,200 square metres of fragrance and cosmetics space together with almost 280 square metres of a stand-alone premium watch shop. Who will shop here, and why not at the airport? King Power's own customer loyalty programme boasts some quarter of a million members and outbound Thai nationals can shop up to 60 days in advance of overseas travel and then collect their purchases airside on departure. It is also worth noting that half of all Japanese who travel to Thailand do so as part of a tour, and this will be another stop on their itinerary.

King Power's commercial grip of Suvarnabhumi Airport is all-encompassing as it also includes foreign exchange and airport

ABOVE The homeware section is set under the natural light provided by the 'open to the sky' roof. This airy feel is further enhanced by the white flooring which runs throughout the retail area of the airport.

RIGHT Topscore, a leisure brand for kids selling everything from sunglasses to footwear.

advertising. Food and beverage, not a King Power speciality, is a joint venture, freeing up the management to concentrate on Duty Free retailing, which is. Part of the King Power approach is also to create their own retail concepts and brands, and this is what marks them out as significantly different from other airports. Tradition has it that an airport, rather like a shopping mall, will have as part of its retail ethos a whole host of local and global retail brands owned and run by their own staff. King Power's vision is that if there is a 'foodie' retail outlet then it should sell everything to do with food, which includes the food itself. A kind of 'acorn to oak to paper to newsprint' scenario. This vision is shared by the two design teams who have helped to create these concept brand stores from interior design through to the graphic communication and name. A good example of this is the Thomas & Tonini concept store that caters for everything to do with food. This is no fly-by-night idea either, because King Power's retail ethos is firmly based on their own market and passenger research and is tailored to what the customer wants at the airport. There is also a luggage store

that has brought together all the major global brands in the market and placed them all under one roof.

For an architecture and design practice like The Design Solution, this type of project presents a totally blank canvas, with no restrictions or creative ideals that have to be inbuilt into the retail design. For the design company and King Power alike the blank canvas is also a tremendous challenge, because whatever is created has to have enough credibility to stand alongside other brands, or else the whole ethos of this particular type of retail offer could fail. A tough call for both parties.

Passenger footfall and flow has been designed so that all the airport entrances – with one exception, and even here the flow does go through Duty Free – are seen as a retail entrance to the Duty Free zone. A passenger cannot avoid it.

The prime retail space is on departure level four, encompassing nearly 7,600 square metres of core Duty Free categories. There are five distinct zones, each with its own design style that complements rather than stands out from the others. By creating these points of difference it is

LEFT Fusion, a store at the very top end of the retail spectrum. The leather handbags are merchandised in a 'precious' way, each set in its own space. High product light levels surrounding the handbags further enhance their perceived 'value'.

TOP RIGHT Moon, a brand created for women, retailing everything from Omega watches through to leather luggage.

BOTTOM RIGHT At Giraffe, the clothes and toys outlet, high light levels have been used at the point of purchase, enhancing the product range. Ambient light is kept to a minimum, thereby allowing the product to be clearly seen.

CROSSING & CONTINENTS

UMI   Samsonite   VICTORINOX

CONNECT

Movies   Music   Digital Camera   Camcorder   Camcorder   Camcorder   CLICK   Accessories   Accessories

hoped that the passengers will move naturally along the entire concourse building, a length of almost a kilometre. What King Power have understood by adopting this design and product grouping policy is that the main reason for being at the airport is not to shop but to fly, so the retail has to be brought a lot closer to the passenger than it would normally be. The first of these five zones is the World of Thailand, which features a 30-metre-long sculpture. Next to this zone are the luxury and specialist retail brand zones. Alongside is the zone housing the Duty Free categories followed by Home and Fashion. In style, although obviously not in configuration, the retail mix is aimed at giving passengers the experience of an upmarket department store.

Part of King Power's comprehensive research programme showed that the traditional core products of beauty, liquor and tobacco still dominate the marketplace for Duty Free, with liquor not surprisingly topping at 23.69 per cent. Fragrances followed at 18.83 per cent and cosmetics at 17.76 per cent.

What makes King Power's operation as the master concessionaire is that all the products sold are actually purchased and owned by King Power rather than the company earnings being based solely on sales turnover. A global brand will put in a person to oversee the operation but the sales are still King Power's. This is a unique way of operating an airport's commercial activity, but one of course which offers far more control of the merchandise on offer, hopefully to the benefit of the passenger. Meanwhile, the brunt of any commercial mistakes is borne by King Power rather than the brand.

One interesting aside is the provision of 'charity shops', which are part of a royal project akin to the Prince of Wales's 'Prince's Trust'. These showcase a variety of charities together with their own product ranges, and earn funds for each.

Bangkok International Suvarnabhumi Airport offers a new way of looking at Duty Free and its potential for enhancing the commerciality of an airport. The fact that it has an off-site but firmly attached airport Duty Free offer downtown is particularly innovative. It represents a commercial challenge not seen before, and one in which everything that is 'retail design' has been pushed to its very limits. An interesting airport venture indeed.

TOP LEFT The Crossing Continents store is a brand specially created by King Power to retail the global luggage brands.

BOTTOM LEFT Connect, a store which retails all items personal and electric, with camcorders a particularly popular purchase.

RIGHT Me – a shop which, as its name suggests, stocks a range of pampering products.

THE ROLE OF THE AIRPORT OPERATOR
CASE STUDY: BAA PLC, UK

Owner: Grupo Ferrovial, Spain

The airport operator is the most critical element in the path to profit for anybody concerned with the business of airports. This is not an over-the-top proclamation – it is reality. It is not so much about power but rather about partnerships, and these are between architects, designers, retailers and a whole raft of different service providers.

BAA plc is now a highly successful UK Stock Exchange listed company with business interests around the globe. It was born out of a government body then named the British Airports Authority that ran seven airports in the UK. The government of the day decided to privatise the body but with a projected reduction in landing fee income – not the ideal way of entering the commercial sector. New and very real income was going to come from the long-term plans both to develop its existing airports and to expand its portfolio by taking on new ones. The commercial aspect of an airport was and is at the very heart of the company. The timing of the company's flot-ation was perfect because the passenger experience at airports at that time was dire. Their immediate priority was to focus on raising standards and choice in retail and the food and beverage offer, which had previously been – and in some airports still is – a generic one with no high-street brands. The passenger was treated as a captive audience with minimal focus on quality, choice or value. Since the mid-1990s, BAA plc have worked consistently to enhance the passenger experience, and in particular have been able through selected retail and catering partnerships to expand their portfolio of brands. These include for the first time brands such as Chanel, Paul Smith, Omega, Tin Goose and Giraffe.

This type of development requires effective specialist experience, and from the outset BAA recruited personnel for both retail and food and drink. Teams were formed that were international in structure and thoughtfully were not about to replicate the high street or shopping mall, but realised that an airport is unique and an exciting arena in which to develop a successful commercial backdrop. The development has been rapid and for retail it has been carried out through a wholly owned subsidiary, World Duty Free (WDF), which operates the company's retail space, its own main stores at each terminal as well as a range of specialist shops including The Cigar House, World of Whiskies, Perfume Gallery, Sunglasses and For Men.

Such has been the commercial success of WDF that BAA plc have been able to sell the concept and management around the world. WDF now manage a number of international operations including the retail and catering offers at a number of US airports, which are non-BAA plc operations.

All this of course could not take place without architects, designers, communications firms, fit-out

TOP The Perfume Gallery. Here the product is king! The merchandise is highly illuminated against a soft background light. Space round the merchandising units is always critical when selling perfume; here there is the added advantage that there is no shop front so the space appears even larger.

BOTTOM The Perfume Gallery. This view of The Perfume Gallery shows the critical split between men's and women's products and then between the brands themselves. This promotes sales amongst the passenger group with limited time as it enables a quick purchase.

ABOVE World Duty Free. Welcome to the World of Duty Free. This is of course airside as opposed to landside. Its huge entrance gives a sense of its importance both to the passenger and to BAA plc themselves. It is a commercial 'pleasure dome'.

TOP RIGHT For Men. It is what it says: 'For Men'. Here there is a clear message hierarchy, making product selection and purchase easy.

BOTTOM RIGHT World Duty Free. There is a striking uniformity of brand application: whatever the company, it is white out of black. This helps to promote continuity of merchandising experience and a better overall look to what could be a visual mishmash if all the brands were allowed to go it alone.

companies and the many other service providers. What BAA plc have done is to put into place a 'preferred supplier list' that covers specialists in a number of areas. These people – and the list is extensive – then work BAA's own design teams in order to meet specific design briefs and develop appropriate design solutions across the airports. This work is both extensive and of a wide variety. It ranges from a major terminal expansion scheme to a small-scale retail store fit-out. For BAA plc this process ensures that all the design projects and solutions are high quality, on time, cost effective, safe and sustainable. For the service providers on the list, those companies know exactly what is required of them and what they will receive in return.

BAA plc estimate that their cosmopolitan audience is around 140 million passengers, including Heathrow, the world's busiest international airport. The diversity of the passenger mix is extensive

and it is estimated that at Heathrow Airport alone there are 120 different nationalities passing through. It is crucial for any potential commercial partner of BAA plc to take this on board, because in order to be an effective partner you need to understand the needs of those passengers. A huge research programme contacted well over a million travellers in the past five years, which has enabled BAA plc to create profiles for each terminal and ensure that with their partners they provide the best-tailored offer for each location. As a partner there is a need to have a solid awareness of the unique environment of an airport. In fact BAA plc shop floor operations are probably the most complex a retailer can experience, but will achieve some of the highest sales densities in the UK – even outperforming Oxford Street! You equally do not have to be big and famous to join the party or have airport experience. Fat Face launched its first ever airport store at Gatwick

THE CIGAR HOUSE

DUNHILL

THE SIGNED RANGE CIGAR

40% OFF SELECTED BOXES OF

EVERYONE CAN BUY

WORLD OF WHISKIES

WORLD OF WHISKIES

BUY 2 SAVE £10 MALT WHISKY

WORLD OF WHISKIES

BUY 2 SAVE £10 MALT WHISKY

TOP LEFT The Cigar House. This is similar to World of Whiskies but with the design going just that step further to enhance the purchasing experience. Here we have wood panelling that goes hand in hand with the traditional cigar shop, aping the old gentlemen's clubs. It is after all still a predominantly male thing.

BOTTOM LEFT World of Whiskies. This type of shop and the working method behind it are what good airport retailing is all about. No searching for brands, they are here and all in one place. This not only helps sales but also lifts the market sector as something special. The design also adds to the whole experience.

ABOVE RIGHT World Duty Free. Here hierarchy is at play. It may say 'Sunglasses' but it also says 'World Duty Free' in a subtle and discreet fashion. Once a passenger has entered the space then it says 'brand'. A clever ploy to remind you that World Duty Free comes first!

South Terminal and it is now one of its top performing outlets in the UK.

It is in the best interests of both parties that the partnership is a success, and to this end BAA plc has a strong marketing policy for the whole airport offer and a number of add-ons to support the passenger, including a no-quibble global guarantee.

Space is always at a premium in an airport, and effective retail and food and beverage masterplanning (see page 100, Retail and Commercial Masterplanning) is critical. BAA plc has adopted a strategy of placing complementary and mutually supportive retail units close together, such as at Heathrow's Terminal 3 where there is a strong cluster of luxury and fashion brands. When floor space permits there is a concentration of food and drink outlets. Customers benefit from both the convenience and the clarity of such a layout.

How do you enter this complex but lucrative marketplace? It is both simple and up front. Concession contracts are normally three to seven

years in length and are turnover related. The concession contracts are underpinned by a minimum guarantee, which is negotiated as a percentage of the previous year's concession payout. All the contracts offer low-cost capital entry to prime sites with no additional payments required for rates, precinct service charge or marketing. BAA's principle appears to be that both partners share the risk and the rewards.

For airport operators such as BAA plc, retail and catering are vital elements in their global operations, not only in delivering the experience the customer wants but also in providing the revenue needed to support any long-term investment programmes. For BAA plc – and it is one of the best airport operators in the business – this approach has enabled them to not only manage seven airports in the UK but also to take significant shareholdings in 12 international airports including Naples, Budapest, Perth and Melbourne. Success obviously breeds success.

DESIGNING FOR THE AIRPORT FOOD MARKET

CASE STUDY: AMSTERDAM SCHIPHOL AIRPORT, LOUNGE ONE, THE NETHERLANDS

Designers: Het Paleis – Menno Rombach, Heineken Inteneural Vies, The Netherlands; Food Court – Jon Sunderland, Sunderland Innerspace Design Inc, Canada; Bubbles – Paul Linse, Studio Linse, The Netherlands

The design and implementation of an airport food and beverage facility over and above a small stand-alone facility is a complex business. It is of course a lot simpler if the airport itself is a new-build project, but even here there are concerns about choice of space, type of environment required, and – probably most importantly – the food itself. For food is fashion and, as we know, fashion can be very fickle. Look at any major city in the world today and there is an abundant choice of culinary delights from wherever in the world one cares to choose. The key thing to remember is that it was not like this 10 years ago and certainly will not be the same in a further 10 years. Imagine having to cope with this state of food and drink flux in an airport, which operates round the clock and has tens of millions of customers passing through it each year. It could prompt the response, 'Let's leave well alone – there are the major brands and they are doing OK.'

As has already been observed, there was one major factor that was cataclysmic for the aviation industry as a whole, and that was 9/11. The subsequent increased security measures caused passenger dwell times to soar. In the wake of the tragic event, faced with the challenge of what to do with such a huge volume of people spending extra time in the airport environment, operators took the pragmatic choice: feed them and sell to them. Fortunately passengers not only returned to flying but also multiplied the times they used the aircraft. We are of course talking about the new phenomenon of the 'low-cost passenger' – a description that does not adequately describe them as the average salary of a person flying with the carrier Easyjet is in excess of £48,000! These are only a few of the market conundrums that face an airport operator, before they even think about the actual design and structure of any new food and drink outlet. For Schiphol Airport these factors were crucial in pre-planning and market research stages. They also had to contemplate major structural changes to the terminal while the passengers travelled through. It is a project rich in positive solutions and creative innovation.

Amsterdam Schiphol Airport has since 1995 had as its master concessionaire HMS Host, a global company well versed in the management of both retail and food and drink facilities at airports. This in itself is worth noting because unlike companies such as BAA plc who can virtually 'own' airports, their investment has to be rolled into the length of any operational contract they have. The catering at Schiphol's Lounge One needed to be upgraded for all the reasons already mentioned, together with a widening of the food

ABOVE Het Paleis as seen from the balcony – a classic brasserie design and layout that celebrates the rich history of Amsterdam.

offer to cope with a broader demographic passenger profile. HMS Host commissioned a series of concepts for the area totalling 10 in all. The two chosen concepts have their roots firmly embedded in the locale: one is called 'City Spirit', and the other 'Het Paleis'. Both of these concepts were designed to cater for all the passenger needs based upon HMS Host's own market research and the obvious timescale constraints of each passenger. This research was critical both to the designs and to the catering facilities.

Three separate time slots had been identified for the food and beverage offer across the board. The '10-minute' person would need refreshment in the 'flow' area, that is to say en route through the terminal to the aircraft. This amount of time predetermines the type of provision, as it has to be a drink with an almost transportable snack. The requirements for this meant the environment could be small, almost bar-like, with no sitting possibilities and limited standing tables. The second passenger group is the '20-minute' slot, for which, because of the added time, the catering area could be away from the 'flow' area but must be easily visible for the passenger to have confidence in using their still limited time to reach it. Here the

food offer could be expanded to both warm and cold meals with the addition of self-service and a seating area. The last group fits 42 per cent of the airport's passenger traffic: those travelling through and using Schiphol as a 'hub', who can have hours between flights and therefore need a more extensive refreshment offer. The area is not visible from the 'flow' and provides an à la carte service for both lunch and dinner with full waiter service. This last area also had to sit comfortably with the other facilities that 'hub' passengers may use, such as the casino.

This research and findings may seem rather obvious but designing, sourcing food and drink products and masterplanning the layout for such a wide sweeping change is complex, particularly where 'fast and fresh' choices for the time-constrained passenger are concerned. By the time all the structural work was finished, Lounge One at Schiphol Airport had grown from 9,000 square metres to 22,000 square metres, with the refreshment areas tripling to 3,000 square metres.

The design policy for the area was also very brave. It would have been simple to appoint a single consultancy to produce all the creative services required, but HMS Host chose the more

LEFT The Het Paleis bar complete with heavily merchandised service station and Thonet-styled tables, chairs and bar stools. A real gem.

RIGHT Lounge One. Ample banquette seating with Amsterdam vignettes.

OVERLEAF The relaxed and informal Bubbles dining area.

ABOVE The Bubbles seating, thoroughly in keeping with the brand both in fun and colour.
RIGHT A glass or two!

difficult route of having a different design practice for each facility. As HMS Host is a global company it was able to call on consultancies that were both local and international, and that is what happened – as Walter Seib, Managing Director of HMS Host, comments:'As a company principle we do not have an internal design team, we look for the very best people wherever they are. This gives us the apparatus to appoint specialists for very special projects and Schiphol Airport Lounge One was a special project for us.'

Special it was, the design and construction of Het Paleis required beams to strengthen the floor as the internal structure itself represented a palace within a palace, the outer 'palace' being the external glass structure of the airport. Het Paleis is a contemporary take on the old 'Crystal Palace' that was situated in the centre of Amsterdam – an environment in which to escape the normal mayhem associated with airport travel. Glass and dark wood are made for each other and in this seafood and wine bar they are majestic. Pass through large Art Deco-influenced glass doors and you could be in some glorious hip city eatery. Detailing is superb, which both emphasises the Het Paleis brand and the contemporary luxury of the environment. The bar is the main focal point with an amazing backdrop of beverages – no need for

trite little pictures here, the product speaks for itself. Tables and chairs are, as you would expect, of Thonet design; and equally reminiscent of bistros all over Europe are the 'Season's Specials' on the chalkboard. The building is monumental and a superb example of what can be provided for the airport's clientele who have that added luxury of time.

Schiphol's other food and drink offers are no less exciting and were no less challenging from a design perspective. Research had shown that the airport was extremely multinational in its passenger traffic, so the offer at the Food Court had to encompass this as its starting point. The designers had to work with an extremely low airport ceiling, which quite literally could have put the court in the shade. Instead the ceiling has been used to successfully brand each separate zone within the area. From Hot Wox to Italian, hot to cold, the court is a veritable world market of fresh food – or, to quote HMS Host,'a festival of food and fun'.

There are two other catering options available, which reflect contemporary life today. The first of these are 'Grab and Fly' outlets on the flow-through, which stock a wide variety of pre-packed products that are sold in special bags for easy carrying to gate or aircraft. There are six such outlets in total, all strategically placed in the airport. Here the design is kept simple, using laminates for the

ABOVE The 'Grab and Fly' shop and quick stop. Well-illuminated and bright in colour, passengers cannot miss it.

construction of the merchandising units. One striking feature of the design concept is that the product range is highly illuminated, attracting the passenger and aiding the 'grab and go' principle. Finally there is Bubbles, for your medium-length break. This seafood and wine bar has those three crucial ingredients in our lives: food, entertainment and retail, complete with a cool atmosphere and chic seats.

An overview of the whole design ethos of Lounge One is one of attention to detail – the little things mean a lot. Chairs are well chosen from a practical point-of-view, and are beautiful as well. Lighting, often a neglected aspect of airport design, is impressive. The whole place works, which is quite a benefit for the eight million or so passengers travelling through the terminal. And the facts and figures only go to show that the approach is a commercially astute one. Prior to Lounge One renovations, annual food and beverage sales in 2003 amounted to 12.4 million euros. The renovations were completed in May 2004, and by 2005 sales had reached 17.5 million euros – an increase of 41 per cent. What concepts, what profits!

ABOVE The Market Food Court with its own extensive branding at the entrance and a good example of how each of the food offers is individually branded: here is Hot Wox.

TOP LEFT One of the food courts, each of which is designed and tailored to show clear individuality.

BOTTOM LEFT The very bright and contemporary Food Court seating area with its spectacular roof.

FROM HIGH STREET TO AIRPORT

CASE STUDY: GIRAFFE, HEATHROW AIRPORT TERMINAL 1, UK

**Franchisee: The Restaurant Group plc,
London, UK**

The catering business is a very complex one in which failures are all too common. It is often perceived as easy – after all, all homes have kitchens … but somebody will pay for what you have cooked. Wrong! The food business is a heady mixture of manufacture and service that are inextricably linked; a great dish can be ruined by poor service, and vice versa, of course. For a food and beverage operation situated on the high street to branch out into the airport sphere is even more fraught with danger. The brand may be extremely well known and respected, successful even, but will it transfer to an airport?

For caterers, the most crucial difference between the high street or shopping mall and the airport is the opening hours. A restaurant might be efficient at producing and serving lunch and dinner on a regular basis, probably only six times a week, but how will it cope 24/7? There is also the issue of product suitability, and in an airport that is critical. Retail brands both large and small have found that retailing in an airport is totally different from the mall. They have either changed both product offer and service, or retired gracefully. For food and drink the same can apply, but there is another option, and that is the use of a franchise: a company willing to invest in a site, run it and share an element of the profits with the brand owner. That is precisely what Giraffe, a leading food and beverage brand in London did to enter Heathrow Airport.

Restaurateur Russel Joffe founded Giraffe back in 1998. The choice of name, according to the founder, suggests 'one who sticks its neck out and goes it alone'. This particular Giraffe is now a herd of 15 and growing all the time, one of its latest being at Heathrow Airport Terminal 1. The brand is both popular and successful and thereby caught the eye of the airport's operator BAA plc. 'Come and join us' was the request, but like so many commercial opportunities in the world the timing wasn't right. It would be a substantial investment in a market that was unfamiliar to the brand. What was right was the style of operation and catering offer. Not quite 'open all hours', but pretty close. Staffing at airports is always a considerable equation: they have to be brand-conscious, and the hours are longer – breakfast starts at five in the morning! In stepped The Restaurant Group plc, a fully quoted restaurant, café, bars and pubs outfit that also has a concessions division. The Restaurant Group plc (TRG), invested the money – and with that, Giraffe stuck its neck into the airport marketplace, albeit with a franchisee. This was not just a question of investment – TRG concessions are a known quantity in the marketplace so there is a degree of confidence in knowing that they will manage the brand in a way Giraffe do on the high street. There was also another reason, as brand owner Russel Joffe commented: 'We do what we do best and for that it is the High Street

ABOVE The Giraffe frontage showing the brand style
of the product listing combined with Giraffe slogans.

...PLEASE WAIT
TO BE SEATED...

ABOVE Keeping the passengers informed!
A row of Giraffe world time clocks situated
above the service hatch.

and managing that expansion.' What Giraffe has gained is another potential profit centre, smaller than a normal operation but still significant and a completely new marketplace into which the brand can be expanded. The management function is TRG concessions and so too is the investment.

It is of course not just one-way traffic; entering into a franchise contract enables Giraffe to learn business from a totally different angle and offers a potentially quicker way to expand into a different marketplace. Giraffe do spend more time at the franchise than they are contracted to do, which is a very sensible approach when you are in an expansionist phase. It is about ensuring that the core brand values that constitute Giraffe are adhered to. This can only come about by constant monitoring and the correct type of training, for as Joffe commented, 'damage to the brand could be horrendous for us so that is why we take the extra time to ensure that all things are right'.

What then of the essentials that make up a restaurant – and in Giraffe at Heathrow Airport it is a 170-cover restaurant? The key brand design was 'engineered' into a tough space restriction that also had to cope with visual constraints. Open sight lines to gates and aircraft necessitated an open front – not much room here for ancillary branding as one would get on the high street. Opening hours are much longer than a normal Giraffe outlet with trade starting at 5.30 am and

going through to 10 pm. The food offer was adjusted, as the airport has no gas facility some of the items such as noodles and wok dishes had to be modified. Ratio of the food offer also changed with a 10 per cent growth in 'Big Breakfast' choice compared with high-street Giraffes.

This is a new and so far successful enterprise for all the parties involved. It has allowed Giraffe to put a toe in the water of a totally new market-place without many of the usual risks. Further expansion on the back of this is now in the pipeline, with a further four or five Giraffes planned across the UK airports. Not all airports are as large or as busy as Heathrow but because of the brand values and the product offer it is feasible to develop smaller concepts and reduce the offer in line with airport passenger numbers. This has the potential to work well in other European air-ports, as the brand becomes better known within the marketplace. The key, like in so many busi-nesses, has been the relationship between those concerned – landlord (BAA plc), franchisee (TRG) and the brand Giraffe.

There are of course other ways to enter the market: a full brand investment approach is the main one, but it is essential to understand that design, implementation, product offer and even delivery of goods need a totally different approach in the airport marketplace. It is exciting but you have to get it right, and that means first time.

ABOVE The 'Light Bar' in all its glory! Bright illumin-ation for a European feel combined with the dark wood of the Orient.

TOP RIGHT Here we see the open bar area together with the doors leading to the secluded but integral smoking area.

BOTTOM RIGHT An image that amply demonstrates the different seating and drinking facilities, from stand up points, bar stools, low lounge chairs to table seating.

lobby style doors which act as a barrier to the smoke. The glass is a visual barrier while maintaining a perfect overall visual harmony for the bar.

The Light Bar serves up a variety of hot snacks so a wider variety of seating and tables was called for. Here The Design Solution were able to source the furniture that would fit their overall design feel locally. As previously mentioned, light is of great importance, and there is a wide variety performing a multi-functional job. The bar as a focal point is highly illuminated with a combination of illuminated product display cases, bar surround ambient lighting and directional spots for the bar surface and back bar operations. This makes for a very brightly lit area so there is a natural spill-over into the rest of the bar. The overall design concept called for a contemporary European bar feel but set within an Asian setting. This is achieved by the use of bamboo flooring and gold leaf behind the bar giving a touch of the locale to it. This whole

design concept was specifically tailored to what the international traveller now expects and is highly stylised as a consequence. Everybody is catered for as Thailand has now become for both leisure and business a popular destination.

It is an airport bar devoid of high street branding so not tied to any corporate look. This is one of the major factors that can allow an airport operator to really push the design boundaries. They also have a 24/7 life so it is important that whatever materials are used in the fit-out are of quality and can stand the test of time. One interesting element to airport bars is that the design is normally either changed or adjusted when the time for a refit comes. This allows the terminal operator to constantly update both style and practical considerations as passenger expectations and needs change. Nothing in an airport, however new and innovative, is for ever. The pace of change is fast.

EMBEDDING A BRANDED BAR DESIGN

CASE STUDY: ARAN, MUNICH AIRPORT TERMINAL 2, GERMANY

Architect: K+P Architects, Munich, Germany

They often say that retail is about 'location, location, location', but the same can be said for food and beverage outlets as well. Space is a very competitive element in airports, especially in newly constructed terminals. Terminal 2 at Munich Airport, designed by Munich-based K+P Architects, has been heralded as a very clear and concise structure, immensely practical for passengers to find their way about, and with the use of a simple but effective small material palette it meets if not exceeds all the criteria for successful terminal design. K+P have a long history not only of designing public spaces but also of masterplanning the interior, a very holistic approach. What the terminal therefore does not need is very heavy-handed brand application, be it retail or food and drink, being forced onto it simply for financial reasons. Here, then, is the potential problem for airport terminals and shopping malls alike: what comes first?

For some time now, shopping malls and retail parks have been assisted by a retail masterplanner, often an architect or design practice, to 'oversee' brand application. Successful airport interiors have a 'design manual' outlining the parameters and requirements of shop design and fit-out within them. The good ones, and most of them are, actually enhance the final finished shop design. In Munich Airport Terminal 2 the same principle applied, not so much about restriction but about brand enhancement.

Although in the UK the word Aran inspires thoughts of the rustic knitwear made on the eponymous Irish islands and so beloved of Ruralists in the 1970s, it was chosen in this case because it is the Celtic expression for bread. It is a simple interpretation for a brand. The name was sourced by the owners at the Museum of Bread Culture in Ulm, Germany. It signifies nature – natural breads devoid of chemicals. Aran have since expanded their product range to include hand-brewed *bier*, sold in branded bottles. In short it is a bar for today's contemporary tastes and beliefs. It is a popular brand in Germany so any watering down or changing of the ethos could pose problems for the business outside of the airport.

Completed in 2003, Aran is situated on Level 05 airside, close to Gates H23–24. Its location is crucial to airport and brand alike. It is in a post-check-in area where international travellers expect a relaxed atmosphere prior to departure. Another of Aran's benefits is that it is well lit from above by natural light and in the central walkway so passengers can either walk around it or into it but they can't miss it! On reflection the location sums up the brand, a 'relaxed' area, 'natural' light and 'central' to passenger flow. This is all added brand value even before service.

Aran's appearance in Terminal 2 was brought about through 'partnerships' with the terminal's architects, the airport itself and the all-important

ABOVE CLOCKWISE General view of the bar; the Aran brand, clear and bold, which acts as the perimeter line of the bar area; Aran 'specials' board which doubles as a merchandising stand for the takeaway products selection; Aran bar sales counter and product display: note the extensive use of wood to complement the 'natural' product range.

Design Committee. This is not to impose draconian measures but to bring out the very best from all concerned. The overall design ethos was really an extension of the existing guidelines for Terminal 1 developed by K+P in collaboration with Büro für Gestaltung Wangler & Abele, thereby promoting consistency across the airport. Aside from the pure functional requirements, the guidelines covered the choice of fittings such as wall and ceiling panels, furnishings and fixtures, and specified that the commercial outlets should have a lightness, openness and transparency of structure – which makes sense given that the ability to see for passengers at airports is key. Existing alongside these physical attributes were the key aesthetic values such as an agreed colour palette. While this may seem daunting for a recognised food and drink or retail brand, in reality the brand's own creativity is able to step up a gear and subtly tweak what they already have on the high street to bring it into another

commercial domain – an airport. It is here, after all, that an international traveller could have his or her first experience of the brand, so a slice of extra brand sophistication would not go amiss.

When it came to a choice of flooring, the terminal already had a grey natural stone, but if that was not thought suitable by the brand then the alternative was wood. The ceiling there is a lot higher than any food and beverage outlet would need, so in Aran's case a very beautiful and effective inverted canopy was used, both holding the space together and providing a focal point.

The first thing you notice about the Aran bar is that it does not appear to be a typical airport food and drink outlet. Its 220 square metres of space are completely freestanding. This has not been forced on the brand to suit the architectural aesthetic of the terminal design, but rather this is the brand's signature method – freestanding units, but generally found in historical buildings.

This fact alone says a lot about the brand: historic buildings do not generally go hand in hand with mass retail or catering. What Aran and the architects K+P had to do was to transport this brand ethos from 'history' as a backdrop into 'the future' in an airport. Aran's bar has no walls, a fact which both aids transparency for passengers and enhances the simplicity of the Aran design. Aran's use of traditional materials such as oak for the flooring, steel for the main structures and glass have produced an open, warm and – from the passenger point of view – inviting atmosphere that happily cohabits with the severity of the airport's own structure surrounding it.

Aran's design work in conjunction with K+P Architects was both challenging and effective. An area had to be developed without any harsh borders, i.e. walls. This was achieved by the flooring alone, the boundaries of the outlet being demarcated by the point at which the wood flooring abuts the grey stone of the terminal. There has been significant use of natural wood: in Aran's case

oak tables and benches of a robust but simple design create the interior.

A unit without walls is a most difficult place to light for it can bleed out into the surrounding area and therefore is not only ineffective but detracts from the area's activity. Here Aran have used a mixture of spot and downlighters both to illuminate the area and to provide a visual, almost subliminal 'entrance' to the bar. The inverted canopy acts as a light diffuser, which is central to the space. All this helps to give prominence to the product with high display illumination and work surfaces for Aran's staff.

Aran's own corporate graphic is much in evidence and acts as a brand 'flag' together with an enclosed element. This is a very good example of how brands can step up to the design challenge of existing within an area that has a totally different function. It forces fresh creative thinking rather than relying on the trusted brand application, and is rapidly becoming *de rigueur* for the new breed of shopping malls.

ABOVE LEFT TO RIGHT Anyone for a latte?; Aran
pastries, a product on which Aran built its business;
Aran boxed chocolates, ready to go.

BELOW An unusual way of packaging chocolate, but in
keeping with the brand.

LEISURE AND WELLBEING

'Flying is tiring! And we all need to be healthy.' This almost sounds like a slogan not to fly but such is the change in people's business and social lifestyles that the need to have enforced downtime and be pampered is now generally recognised. Leisure and wellbeing facilities are everywhere: go to a gym and along with weights there are also toning tables. Stay at a city centre hotel and you will find facilities are in the basement. Facial massages used to be a girl thing; now all of us are complete with a bronze glow. How has this come about, and why has the travel business taken to it with such gusto? The simple truth is that it is neither fad nor fancy, it has been with us for quite some time and in certain parts of the globe it is endemic in the culture.

International carriers, especially long-haul ones, now regularly dispense wellbeing packs to business class passengers as a matter of course. They may only contain moisturisers, eye refreshers and the like but passengers love them and use them. Some carriers have taken this a step further by opening wellbeing facilities within their own lounges, and again these prove popular. Whatever has happened to 'grin and bear it'? One carrier will have none of this stiff-upper-lip nonsense so beloved of the British – they want to care for you both before and after you have flown with them. I am referring to Virgin Atlantic, headed by the almost divine figure of Sir Richard Branson. Virgin started their 'Clubhouse' facility some time back and over the last few years it has been kept constantly updated to serve the changing demands of its passengers. Out has gone the golf, in have come the spray-tanning booths. This of course is not just about simple change; design has to be employed so everything appears just that one step ahead of its competitors. Virgin takes this offer very seriously, investing millions of pounds on a continual basis. There is of course the ubiquitous bar but even this is different, and that difference is the Virgin brand – it is a bar but it's a Virgin bar!

What then have the actual airports done in this growing marketplace, and who are the players? A company called Rejuve has opened a wellbeing clinic at Heathrow Airport's Terminal 1 building. The owners are not leisure entrepreneurs but actual passengers who thought the idea a good one and put their money behind the project. A brand has been created and the health and wellbeing

ABOVE Rejuve, Heathrow Airport Terminal 1. The lighting 'trees' in the reception area provide both ambient light and a visual focus. They came about due to restrictions in the suspension of lights from the ceiling, but the result has been to turn a negative into a positive.

LEFT Virgin Clubhouse, Heathrow Airport Terminal 3. The exterior seating to the main bar area. The banquettes are supplemented by the Charles Eames chairs with brightly coloured side tables, adding a visual focus.

ethos taken a step further. There are similarities with the non-airport world in that a passenger books for whatever service they require and can even join the club. Here both interior and lighting design are equally important. The atmosphere is critical to providing the right ambience for each separate facility and activity. All the various elements have been successfully integrated, and that is the strength of the design.

Extra facilities for passengers are not all about pampering: for a lot of the regular passengers, business is the name of the game and it is here once again that design has led innovation. Business lounges used to be very undemocratic affairs reserved for the brilliantine pin-striped man. Fortunately he has retired and they have opened their doors to the odd millionaire in jeans and trainers – whatever next? As a consequence of this the design and management of business lounges have changed. Technology has also contributed but it is the overall picture that is important. One of the most advanced and exciting business lounge concepts is for Lisbon Airport. The provision is extensive and so the design skills needed for the area are above what is normally needed. They have been traditionally small out-of-the-way places, more to do with power points and telephone jacks than centred in the airport for all to see and use.

Hub airports are a natural habitat for leisure and wellbeing facilities. It makes sense as a passenger can spend up to eight hours waiting for the follow-on flight. Hubs are now providing hotel rooms by the hour, cinemas, games rooms and even rooftop gardens and swimming pools. One such airport is Singapore Changi Airport, where these extra facilities have been designed and developed over a long time. It is a leisure paradise with a feeling of space, thereby promoting a more relaxed mood for the passenger.

Space is critical for any airport's advancement into this market. Most European airports have a problem fitting all the retail and catering requirements into the building envelope. Of course design can help, and it is seen as critical in this marketplace, but even the best design solutions cannot make up for lack of space. Rooftops are an obvious starting point. The fact that the facilities on offer are for passengers with time to spare means that these places are a destination stop. Passengers will seek them out.

LEFT Rejuve, Heathrow Airport Terminal 1. The circular domed roof is one of the main focal points and serves to cover up the terminal's metal structure. Lighting Design House, responsible for all the lighting design at Rejuve, have created these chandelier-styled lights to enhance the luxury feel of the lounge.

RIGHT Business Lounge, Lisbon Airport. The bar in all its majesty! There will be uplighters, downlighters, wireless points for those executives who insist on working and the bar for the more relaxed passenger.

brands and personalities. The full spa offer is very extensive and includes beauty rooms, a Jacuzzi, sauna facilities and even a spray-tanning booth. For their hair salon Virgin Atlantic teamed up with New York's elite chain of salons Bumble and bumble, which allows both brands to complement each other. The salon has the ambience akin to that of a five-star hotel club. It is not all about a 'wellbeing' lifestyle – for a good majority of people 'wellbeing' can equal indulgence, which gives another slant to the term. Next to the spa facilities are the naughty bits – watching a movie while concentrating on chocolate or popcorn, and the star attraction in the main lounge area, the Bar. At 14 metres in length, you can't miss it. For anybody catching the evening flight to JFK Airport this is a must, especially for the lone businessperson. A cocktail and a chat with the barman – a traveller's creed wherever you are!

The recruitment of brands such as Bumble and bumble was not a one-off event: as the facility has evolved, Virgin Atlantic have been very astute at recruiting people at the very top of their game. The Clubhouse has a full service restaurant offering whatever a passenger requires, whether it's shepherd's pie or something a little more exotic. Mark Hix, Chef-Director of both Le Caprice and The Ivy restaurants in London, was brought in as a consultant to work on menu development as well as food style and kitchen requirements. To complement this à la carte offer there is also a deli counter for those a little less hungry. At first glance this all may seem a little indulgent – celebrity chefs and full service – but it is underpinned by both practicalities of transatlantic flight and time issues. For a lot of Virgin's passengers their preference is to eat before they board so that the in-the-air time can be spent sleeping.

Part of the lounge area design has involved the creation of a roof garden that not only is near the plane park but also required a significant amount

RIGHT The play area complete with pool table and wide-screen TV. During daylight hours the pool table has the benefit of natural light from above which is supplemented by two halogen strip lights.

BELOW An overall view of the Clubhouse facility detailing the wooden floor and the ceiling uplighters which provide the main reflective light source. Note the 'Riva' speedboat-styled banquette seating.

ABOVE The laptop bar comes complete with foliage! Here additional lighting is provided by a row of down-lighters within the shades.

of natural light. This rather more leisure-based element operates on both an inside-out and outside-in principle. This area was known as the 'Conservatory' but has now been renamed the 'Sky Lounge'.

There is a further facility, that of the boys' 'Den'. This has all the toys such as snooker, Space Invaders and a plethora of computer games that would keep a 'techy' going for weeks, and the list goes on – even a kids' area is provided. Virgin businesspeople start young!

Retail masterplanning at airports is a science in itself but what has been designed and configured into 230 square metres is a tribute to the Softroom architecture studio and Virgin Atlantic's own design team, and here is that extra value. As Virgin is such a large and diverse commercial entity, ideas and solutions can come from the group as a whole – be it music, travel, retail,

finance or leisure clubs. All these commercial pieces work off the background of 'service'. With this comes the phenomenal inherent ability to self-promote, amounting to a very powerful force. Virgin Atlantic talks about its own passengers' 'brag factor' – their sense of one-upmanship over other airlines. With this comes customer loyalty, which allows Virgin Atlantic to predict a 10 per cent growth factor over the next few years precisely because of the design and provision of the Clubhouse.

The layout of the whole of the Virgin passenger facility enables a simple and speedy throughput. If the passengers feel this then they are relaxed and have the ability to utilise fully what is on offer. From spas to the bar and all the bits in-between, it is an airline passenger facility unsurpassed in both design and offer – what comes next?

BRANDING AND DESIGN OF WELLBEING CLINICS
CASE STUDY: REJUVE, HEATHROW AIRPORT TERMINAL 1, UK

Architect: The Design Solution, London, UK
Lighting Consultant: Lighting Design House, London, UK

Wellbeing facilities are well and truly the new kids on the block. There have been hair salons and the like, but places such as Rejuve at Heathrow Airport Terminal 1 represent a turning point in the provision of yet further passenger facilities. Frankly it is a wonder that there is any space left in any world airport to offer a further marketplace. Space is at the heart of the matter but so is 'lifestyle', a word that seems to mean anything to anyone. It is lifestyle that has driven global health issues; smoking is out and drinking should only be done in moderation. What is there left to do? The answer lies in places such as Rejuve – look after ourselves, become more health-conscious and look good. It is a complete lifestyle turnaround and there is a no more punishing procedure than being a frequent flyer. It is stressful and it takes its toll. BAA plc, operators of Heathrow Airport, are at the forefront in pushing the parameters of passenger facilities, and it is to 'lifestyle' as a market offering that they have gone. Out has gone the mezzanine bar and in has come wellbeing – and in this case it is Rejuve.

The idea for Rejuve came from a group of frequent-flyers-turned-investors. Designing and implementing such a project required airport know-how on a commercial scale as well as brand-building experience. Rejuve appointed the

London-based architecture and design company The Design Solution to create the 'clinic'. The Design Solution have a significant history of commercial masterplanning in airports around the globe together with the design of individual airport retail units. It was because of this that the directors of Rejuve selected the company.

The design brief was open from a creative standpoint but targeted at the frequent flyers. It was to be an area that had the potential to relax as well as to stimulate – a total rejuvenating experience. Also Rejuve was to act as both a retailer of related products and a provider of healthy food and beverage; all this had to be encapsulated into the design. Rejuve is not for the one-time passenger: it is firmly aimed at the frequent flyer, and to this end the atmosphere had to have as its basis a club-like feel. Passengers join Rejuve either at the venue or online.

The Design Solution evolved the centre's design over a few months as the 'club's' visual format came about. Think of clubs and they are either sports clubs with a medicinal feel or gentlemen's clubs with a faded elegance that has passed into decay. Rejuve wanted something that had a feel of history but was also quirky. The design was to be based on pure theatre and drama, with the designer citing the film *Theatre of Gentlemen* as

ABOVE The entrance to the club lounge via the treatment rooms corridor.

OVERLEAF A padded leather panel wall was constructed, here seen in a greyish hue. This hides the electrical system that provides both power and telecommunications points, seen on the walls. The chairs are a Philippe Starck design purchased 'off the peg', with the clever practical element of only having one arm, thereby freeing up the other side of the chair to the side table.

LEFT This is the 'club lounge', a design style updated with luxury rather than faded elegance. The purple carpet was specially made with the corporate identity of the Rejuve company. The iconic panels, designed by Peter Woodward, take their inspiration from Greece, with each panel representing a mythological figure. Red leather panelling is used to cover the wall of a treatment room.

RIGHT Here Rejuve have ensured that even the computer terminals enjoy a relaxing atmosphere with a backdrop of red leather panelling and olive wood flooring.

inspiration. A rich palette of materials has been used, including marble and walnut. Timber is used for flooring – a light olive ash in the reception area. Colours are also rich, incorporating deep purple and blues together with the traditional club use of brown.

Design is ideally about working successfully with a proactive and intelligent client. With Rejuve there were three parties actively involved in promoting the overall look. Apart from the architectural practice The Design Solution and client Rejuve there was also BAA plc, the airport operators. The scenario, and it is a good example of how things should be, was that Rejuve presented their overall concept to BAA plc and The Design Solution presented the creative work to them also. Everybody knows what to do and also what is required from an airport point of view, which is critical because an airport terminal is not a high street.

It is easy to appreciate how Rejuve looks, but the design work was also about floor planning. Where was the massage table going to be? How many treatment rooms would be needed? What shower facilities should be provided? And where would the barber be situated? This in itself is a very complex job because it is not only about placement but also concerns the correct assumptions for passenger usage of each separate facility. These facilities and the whole Rejuve spa have also to be lit, and lit appropriately for each separate function. The company that provide the solutions is Lighting Design House, who carried out a significant amount of research into just what lights were required where and also the different effect of colour on those activities.

Completed in 2006, Rejuve is on a mezzanine level and has no determinable natural light. It was crucial that good-quality light was provided, and for this tungsten halogen as an overall technology

LEFT In the massage suites the mahogany-finish walls help ensure continuity of materials and design throughout the area. Here it is complemented by a humorous ceramic tile panel designed by Peter Woodward.

RIGHT Mahogany-finished panelling is used again in the hairdressing facility. The mix of materials is further complemented by the use of white marble on the floor and ceramic basins.

was the preferred option. One part of the lighting requirement was to allow the distinction between daytime and evening, so patterns were applied to achieve this. As Rejuve is about both relaxation and stimulation, the treatment rooms had to have a light source that could aid these moods. Research showed that red light actually relaxes the body while blue light does the reverse. This is opposite to what a layperson might expect but shows how holistic the total planning, design and execution process was for the Rejuve offer. The reception area, which includes the Juice Bar, had limitations on the use of lights: no suspended lights could be employed, and the lamp brightness had to be at a higher level. Add to this airport terminal compliance for wiring and fusing and the whole lighting programme is a significant and successful achievement.

The airport terminal provision of facilities such as Rejuve is set to grow; it has become part of 'lifestyle' life. What are shown in the Rejuve project are the benefits of good working partnerships and the design and planning complexity of such places.

ABOVE If one must! The Rejuve wellbeing clinic comes complete with a gym. The flooring is rubber, which absorbs the noise for the commercial unit situated below on the ground floor. Entry is via a glass door in the treatment facilities corridor.

OVERLEAF The Rejuve reception area complete with olive wood floor. This area has three main functions: booking passengers in, retailing rejuvenating products, and a health bar. The merchandising unit acts as a focus for the retail offer.

DESIGN FOR BUSINESS LOUNGES
CASE STUDY: BUSINESS LOUNGE, LISBON AIRPORT, PORTUGAL

Designer: Barber Design Consultants, London, UK

Business lounges are a critical element in any passenger terminal these days, and especially so in airports. In theory they are a place set apart from the general service areas such as retail and food and drink. They are a place where the global work ethic of executives can continue unabated.

How does design help? Frankly, at its bluntest it keeps the business lounge in a contemporary setting. This is not about pretty colours on the latest plasma gizmo, but being up to date with the needs of those for whom these lounges must now cater. In the words of Doug Barber of Barber Design, 'the traditional marketplace for business lounges was the well-suited business gent in his 50s or 60s. They have now all retired, what you have today is a 28-year-old dressed in trainers and jeans, who drives an Aston Martin and is worth several million. While that is perhaps not commonplace it gives an idea of how business lounges have to or will have to evolve, and that is before talking about the increasing numbers of ladies using the facilities.'

What Barber is saying is that barriers have to be broken down. There can be no differentiation nowadays between the corporate person and the entrepreneur. Things have to be more democratic, pin stripes and ties are fine but jeans and trainers must also be catered for. Traditionally the business lounge has always been behind closed doors,

almost a secret location. Nowadays any overall design approach to a business lounge must be based around it being more welcoming and appealing. The main obstacle to this is that the majority of these places are either run by or affiliated to a particular carrier rather than an airport operator. What has now happened, as global business has evolved ever faster, is that the profile of the businessperson has changed – and this needs to be designed into any plan for a business lounge. They are no longer old boys' clubs!

The design project for Lisbon Airport, begun in 2006, was going to be adventurous from the start as its size was considerably larger than the normal two to three hundred square metres. Making it attractive and open was essential, but the design had to take into account that it is a destination zone for the business traveller. The style chosen – one which is now a favourite for hotel reception areas – is that of a 'club lounge', a space away from the hustle and bustle. The design brief stipulated what was required on a practical level – six meeting rooms, one double meeting room, a bar, a central chill-out area, hot spots, and a reception area. The reception area was critical to the success of the business lounge as it was situated at ground level with the lounge a floor above. Part of the overall design allowed the concept of 'openness' to be fully appreciated by placing some of the

ABOVE This graphic shows the bar area. The walls are plastered with a polymer finish. This simple solution counterbalances the deep-pile luxury of the crimson carpet that will be installed. All the lighting has adjustable levels so that different moods can be created for different times of the day. The dark grey marble-topped bar adds to the simplicity. The graphic panels hide the speakers that provide the background music.

RIGHT Plan.

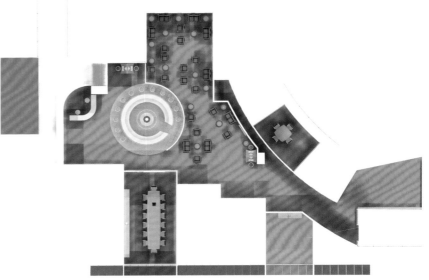

lounge facilities next to a small balcony overlooking the retail and catering area below, thus keeping the business passenger in touch with the rest of the airport and not shut away.

As with most 'club lounges', luxury of materials is key to its success and for the business traveller a standard that is expected. Here the design incorporated deep pile carpets in some areas and black granite in others, this due to not only 'luxury' but also the practical element of usage. A selection of wood finishes was also incorporated and a choice of classic furniture chosen around the style of Le Corbusier so as to appear contemporary but undated.

The choice of colours is very important for a business lounge and the colour palette now moved towards and encompassed the new business traveller with trainers. It would have been easy to stay with the hotel club lounge colour chart, but the influences come from another airport activity, that of retail. In retail the right choice of colour will help people stay in the store longer, whereas the wrong choice has the opposite effect – they leave. The colour palette chosen was a selection of what the designer termed 'funky, but not in-your-face', a feeling of a contemporary atmosphere that was both welcoming and appealing.

Workability is important, as although it may be termed a 'lounge' it is in fact a multi-purpose suite that has to answer all business needs. These can range from a much-needed refreshment in a relaxed atmosphere to a full-blown board meeting. Layout for this design project was critical. The appealing sections of the business lounge offer were placed at the front of the area so as to be visible from the exterior. Hardcore meeting rooms and business areas were located at the rear. The bar was a central theme, complete with soft low seating in the chill-out areas. As with retail, lifetime equations are critical: here the design, use of materials and probably even more importantly what a business lounge will need to be in the future, added up to a five-year cycle. It is a simple, practical and contemporary design which satisfies the needs of today and the near future.

One question in all of this has to be: what about technology? All business nowadays has to use and cope with it. For some it is the 'emperor's new clothes' syndrome, but we all live with it. Broadband is critical to business lounges so that a person can hook up and be in touch. Wireless hotspots were also built into the design, as were plasma screens. The advent of wireless technology has been an enormous help to business lounges and businesspeople. For the operator and investor of a business lounge, it keeps the technology costs down. As this variety of communications technology advances, so it appears to get both smaller and cheaper. This is important for the design of future lounges: versatility is key, and if areas can adjust to technology as it becomes available and its use widespread, then business lounges in all passenger terminals will thrive.

LEFT The roof graphic line dictates the way through in an almost subconscious manner. The immediate bar area is designed to have aluminium side panels, with black slate tiles next to the bar, before heading off into the luxury of carpet.

TOP LEFT The bar in all its majesty! There will be uplighters, downlighters, wireless points for those executives who insist on working and the bar for the more relaxed passenger.

ABOVE LEFT The selection of the Le Corbusier chairs provides not only superb seating but also a visual balance to the austerity of the walnut-panelled walls. This boardroom comes complete with the ubiquitous plasma screen.

TOP RIGHT Lisbon Airport. The reception area with its lift entrance directly up from the airport terminal. The frosted glass wall hints at what is on offer in this business lounge.

ABOVE RIGHT Another similar situation but here the glass wall provides a view of the main airport and a runway.

LUXURY BRANDS

Luxury by definition refers to the inessential: any commodities or services that are beyond our basic needs. Denoting pleasure and comfort, it can also have connotations of expense and even decadence. Thus while for many, luxury represents something to aspire to and take enjoyment in, for others it reeks of conspicuous consumption and sumptuous living. There can be no doubt, though, that in the business environment of airport retail, the expanding luxury market can only be regarded as positive. The provision of luxury, in terms of both products and services, has been a growing phenomenon for the last five years and one for which there is a heightened passenger demand. With globalisation, luxury services and goods – as well as travel – have become more affordable for the most affluent sector of society; this has coincided with a period of global wealth when the rich have tended to get richer in countries with booming economies, such as the US, the UK, China and India.

The birth of the luxury brand both on the high street and in the airport has grown out of what has for centuries been one of the cornerstones of the luxury goods trade, alongside drink and tobacco – perfume. To be a luxury brand, a company or product range has not only to produce a majority of luxury goods, but also to have a name that evokes quality and is thus identifiable with luxury itself. Perfume is a product that gives itself perfectly to the embodiment of a brand name, whether it is that of a fashion house – such as Chanel, Christian Dior or Chloé – or a celebrity name like the Beckhams'; scents can be blended and their packaging designed to resonate with a specific brand or personality.

Since the earliest days of air travel, perfume has also been a favourite airport purchase, an indulgence that has the added benefit of being tax-free when bought airside. For the passenger it represents value for money: a spot of luxury at a discounted price. For the airport operator the revenue is significant. Today the branding of luxury perfumes and aspiring luxury perfumes has become even more important, for a perfume can make the brand more money than the clothing range. This is especially the case with ladies' perfumes. There are some haute-couture fashion houses that actually run at a loss and are entirely shored up by their perfume sales. Their prestigious flagship fashion

ABOVE Harrods, Heathrow Terminal 1. The lighting of the sign gives it a contemporary look, so essential in airport retailing. The shop's interior and merchandising units are similar to those of its London store, as is the range of products on display.

LEFT The very strong Mulberry brand image on display in the "Luxury" retail offer.

ABOVE Links, Heathrow Terminal 1. This luxury-brand store has made good use of its core identity in the interior design and layout together with the colour palette. The shop's exterior uses a 'new' approach to airport retailing by adopting a semi-protruding sign. This both enhances the brand and acts as a more visual signpost for the retailer.

outlets and international catwalk shows give them vital visibility and presence in the world's media and are thus in a sense extended marketing activities for brand building.

The question facing airport operators once the popularity of perfume as an airport purchase had been firmly established was therefore how to expand the retail offer on a profit-making basis. The answer was high-end luggage, together with 'accessories' in all shapes and sizes. Initially the range of goods was narrow and they were merchandised very much as part of a large Duty Free offering, sold from a simple product stand devoid of any coherently branded presentation.

Out of this warehouse-like retailing method has come a huge commercial phenomenon. Out have gone stands and in have come shops and stand-alone high-octane boutiques. These vary greatly in size, depending on the goods on offer and the space available. A good track record of sales in other airports will also help. Some brands such as Mulberry have purposely limited their selection to small but high-price products and have left their clothing range 'at home', therefore limiting the space they require. E-shopping is also enabling luxury brands to sell more of their range as travellers can purchase items at the airport with the tax reduction and have them delivered to their residence, again keeping the store size requirement down.

Store design is critical for any brand, but especially so for the luxury ones; and there are several issues that have to be considered with regard to aiport retail design that differ from the high street. Firstly, there are the many and stringent safety regulations that are airport specific. Then there is the number of different parties that are involved. In general, the airport operator will have an appointed architectural practice that governs the retail framework on its behalf. In addition there is the terminal operator who heads up the various parties concerned. This may at first seem daunting for the manager of a luxury brand, who is used to maintaining absolute control of the presentation of their products, but it is crucial for them to understand that this kind of retailing is different and to adapt the brand's retail design accordingly. After all, it is in the airport operator's best interests to position a particular brand in the right place and then to ensure, through their appointed architect, that the brand design is not watered down but enhanced by the airport environment.

The range of products has also grown and continues to expand, as does the retailing methodology. There are now shops selling everything from fine clothes to cut-glass ornaments. The number of luxury brand retailers is also increasing within the airport retail offer. An international traveller can enter an airport precinct and be presented with the very same exclusive names found on Bond Street in London, Rue St Honoré in Paris, 5th Avenue in New York or the Via dei Condotti in Rome.

The fact that luxury and the selling of it is a truly international activity has also suited the transient airport environment. It has allowed for brand recognition across a wider range of nationalities. The cult of celebrity, in particular, has given global brand activity a significant commercial boost. Though this has been around since the rise of the film star in the 1950s, the last decade has seen it intensify. Celebrity has been used in a much more focused and targeted way by companies, creating an important badge of association for products. The right celebrity endorsement can ensure that a brand remains fresh, distinct and alluring on the international market. Mulberry has been very successful at attracting both stars and celebrities to its product stable. Brooke Shields uses her 'Brooke' bag, which was not even named after her; and Kate Moss is regularly photographed clutching her Mulberry bag. Rather like a top-flight Formula One driver who, prior to receiving the winner's trophy, will ensure that he puts on his personal sponsor's watch, and check that all the companies' names are clear on his overalls or 'race wear', so luxury clothing brands will 'retain' certain people to wear only their label. What is important for the luxury brand is to live up to the ambience and maintain a level of exclusivity through price, quality and product.

With the growth in luxury brands has come the ability for companies in this sector to test new areas in the world without going through the very high cost of opening on the high street or in the shopping mall. Of course, it is not simply a question of choosing the nearest airport: the right passenger profile is essential. Luxury brands that are predominantly global will sell best in international hub airports where there are a large number of business travellers passing through. An airport operator such as BAA plc will regularly collect data on the habits of its passengers with regard to retail

LEFT BOSS, Heathrow Terminal 1. The luxury German brand has specialised in its womenswear range rather than its entire clothing line for this Heathrow outlet. The store is open-fronted and well illuminated, with accessories displayed at the back of the shop, thereby drawing people in.

and provide these statistics for the brands to study. This process assists product selection for the store, as well as informing where a store should be positioned and what its size should be. The French brand Chloé has recently opened its first store in Singapore, and mirrored the presence by opening up in Changi Airport. While at present it is largely Western brands that are being exported globally, there are signs that this is set to change. Shanghai Tang, an Asian aspiring luxury brand, has been able to attract a considerable amount of business from European travellers in its stores in Asian airports. What is critical to all the world's luxury brands is that the brand communication is not altered, even in passenger terminals; otherwise the brand could be damaged irreparably in that part of the world. This has been a challenge both to the brands themselves and also to the terminal operators who want to attract them. One solution has been to group all the luxury global brands together. A successful example of this is Changi Airport, where the Asian trading group Valiram have presented the brands in an almost self-contained unit but with multiple entries and a free passenger flow-through. This 'centre' is a further design step in the airport market, as Julian Levy of Valiram commented: 'We have stand-alone luxury shops but this is the way forward: all the brands together, specifically targeted at the right clientele and situated in the right place. The whole area is clear and defined.' All the brands have an identity which is recognisable to the cognoscenti and helps to make this a true luxury brand experience for the passenger.

Just as the proliferation of luxury brand retailing can be seen to have its seeds in the sales of duty-free perfume, the successful positioning of luxury brands in the airport context is set to spawn a whole new range of luxury services. The 'celebrity' American chef Todd English has opened a restaurant in LaGuardia Airport, New York, called Figs. It is, as he comments, 'for customers with enough time before their flight to sit down and enjoy a meal they would be having in Manhattan'. London's Heathrow Terminal 5 will have a Gordon Ramsay restaurant when it finally opens. 'Best of the Best' is a luxury lottery brand that specialises in high-end motor vehicles, offering the possibility of winning a Bentley car or a Ducati motorbike for the purchase of a significantly priced ticket. Singapore Airport even has its own 'luxury terminal', providing pampering and protection that includes a chauffeur-driven car from terminal to plane.

Where could luxury lead us? Bespoke designer clothing would be the ultimate. What about a Philip Treacy hat – measured for on the way out and fitted after in-bound?

As Robbie Gill of The Design Solution in London commented, 'with the increasing dominance of brands in airports, "Luxury" is fast becoming one of the most important': it has the potential, provided that it is located in the right place, to earn more per square metre than conventional airport retailers. It is of course reliant on affluent passengers. The rise in global commerce means that more businesspeople will travel, and unless there is a global downturn, the future should be promising. It must be remembered nonetheless that all international airports need a balanced retail offer – that is, something for everyone.

FAR LEFT Mulberry. American actress Brooke Shields carrying with her a Mulberry bag curiously named 'Brooke'. A coincidence, apparently!

LEFT Mulberry. British model and celebrity Kate Moss with her Mulberry bag. Celebrity endorsement is very important to luxury brands, as it gives credibility by association. In the UK at least, Moss's celebrity status has exceeded her modelling fame, as this paparazzi photograph taken on a London street indicates.

ABOVE Burberry, Heathrow Terminal 1. The large, wide shop complements the brand identity by using light-coloured wood. The 'second' entrance acts as a magnet to the softer interior at the back of the unit.

LEFT Chanel, Heathrow Terminal 3. The shop, a corner unit, is clearly 'signed' by the dark, open door surround which is then echoed in the counters and merchandising units. Once again for a luxury brand the products are clearly on display but with security as an essential element.

PROJECTING AND ENHANCING A LUXURY BRAND
CASE STUDIES: BULGARI, HARRODS AND OTHERS, WORLDWIDE

A luxury brand has a huge commercial value running into millions if not billions of dollars. This value has been built up over decades and sometimes several generations of the same family. When a luxury brand appoints a design company to redesign or extend the commerciality of its business, the design company becomes the 'brand guardian', making sure that any changes, be they to the products themselves or to the communication of their identity, truly reflect what the brand stands for.

Airport retail is very different to the high-street environment. The outlets generally do not have shop fronts, and they also have to conform to various rules and regulations that are necessary in the aviation world. This can come as something of a shock to companies contemplating a venture into airport terminals, and for a luxury brand it can be particularly unsettling. In addition, there is the issue of the design of the airport itself. Was it conceived as both a commercial and infrastructure entity, or merely as a transport- and people-processing facility? This makes a considerable difference in terms of both availability of space and retail layout. Luxury brand retailers will often have a limited number of products, but an extended range of each. Sunglasses are not generally sold on the high street in winter, but they are in an airport.

Also, an airport outlet has the potential to display a brand in all its glory to a thoroughly international marketplace – especially if it is airside. For this factor alone it is vital that the brand gets its message right.

The basis for good luxury brand communication starts with its relationship with the terminal operator. This is critical and depends on a few crucial elements. Some airport operators are actually authorities which may not have been particularly responsive to retailing needs in the past. Thankfully this is now changing rapidly. The rule generally is that the greater the level of private ownership, the greater the level of communication between the airport and the commercial activities going on in the terminals. An airport operator such as the UK-based BAA plc has been very proactive in promoting luxury brands as part of its commercial offer to passengers.

Another important factor is the positioning of the retail outlet within the wider context of the terminal, and this is down to the architectural practice that is carrying out the exercise. Positioning generally relates to calculated flow data of demographic types through the space. In simple terms, both airport operator and luxury brand owners like to be close to the long-haul gates as this makes commercial sense for the

ABOVE Bulgari, Athens International Airport. The beautiful curved and open front is a perfect example of the kind of modern luxury retailing design that is so essential in an airport.

ABOVE Zegna, Venice Marco Polo International Airport. This is luxury with a capital 'L'. What store design. What luxury brand presence. Despite the open front, the store is different from the passenger concourse in every way.

luxury brand with regard to passenger profile. In some cases, though, the airport layout is more centralised with a single international departures lounge, the same gates being used for both short-haul and long-haul flights, so the passenger profile is constantly changing.

Once a site has been selected, it is then up to the luxury brand to work closely with the airport's architect-designers to both maximise commercial potential and protect the hard-earned brand values. This can be tricky due to the particularities of the airport retail environment. On the high street, luxury brands tend to place a greater emphasis on the exterior door and window configuration, using it to 'protect' and 'promote' the brand rather than as a welcoming facility. The lack of shop fronts at airports therefore presents a particular challenge. For the luxury brands it is also a difficult balance, as they are not 'general' retail and their price point is significantly higher. Again a compromise has to be found, and here the airport operators' architect-designers are well versed in answering difficult brand problems. Steve Collis, Managing Director of JHP Design who were responsible for the master-plan of Venice Marco Polo International Airport explains:

You could argue that standard retailers are more inclined to listen to the airport in terms of adapting their store design to suit. They treat the airport as a different environment and will have open shop fronts which make it easier for customers to shop. Some luxury retailers still try to dictate and open the same store that you would see on the high street; at Venice Marco Polo International Airport the Bulgari brand has an open shop front and they have fully understood the implications of airport retailing in their shop design. It is open, fresh, and easy to navigate. It is also unmistakably Bulgari. Another store design which suits airport retailing is the Harrods store,

RIGHT Harrods, Heathrow Terminal 1. The outlet has an open front but is still reminiscent of the Harrods Knightsbridge store's facade. It has 'signed' two other luxury brands as additional enticement for passengers to enter.

BELOW La Perla a true luxury lingerie brand!

ABOVE LEFT A glimpse of the nature of luxury brand environments, made different by good use of different materials.
ABOVE RIGHT Elite Travel Retail, the name says it all!
BELOW Bottega dei Sapori, Venice Marco Polo International Airport. This store is an example of the kind of high-spec interior that is essential for luxury merchandise.

the front is open with product on display
but it still has the essential luxury brand
qualities of its store exterior.
In designing a luxury brand outlet in an airport, it
is essential for the different shape of the unit in
comparison to a high street store to be taken into
account. Whilst high street shops tend to have a
relatively narrow front and a deep space within, in
an airport it is the opposite. The rationale behind
the shallowness of airport retail outlets is to avoid
the customer missing flight announcements while
browsing at the back of a store. This is also the reason behind the open store fronts, which have the
added benefit of giving a more welcoming
impression. If a luxury brand does enclose the
front, even in glass, there is a potential for keeping

interested passengers out and creating stress for
those inside. What luxury brands have to realise is
that openness does not 'devalue' their brand. If the
brand feels the need for 'borders', this effect can be
created in a subliminal fashion by the imaginative
use of flooring to differentiate the retail space
from the concourse.

Luxury brand managers need to understand
that airport retail is different from other parts of
their business; but they may rest assured that the
airport's architects-designers will actively set out
to assist in the re-expression of the brand personality in the airport environment. Luxury brands
themselves will need to relate to the airport environment in order to get the best out of it.

ABOVE Swatch, Venice Marco Polo International
Airport. Is Swatch a luxury brand? Increasingly so as it
moves up a product gear. It is crucial to have the brand
message and store design to go with it, though – and
Swatch certainly seems to have achieved this here.

THE LUXURY BRANDS SHOPPING CENTRE
CASE STUDY: VALIRAM, CHANGI AIRPORT TERMINAL 2, SINGAPORE

Architect: The Design Solution, London, UK

Changi Airport has always been at the very fore-front of service for airport users. Passengers list it as 'Best Airport in the World' year on year, and for many different reasons. For the last few years it has won the Diamond Award from the magazine *Buying Business Travel*, and for five years it has been named 'Top Worldwide Airport' by the publication *Wanderlust*, so it is easy to see that it caters for all sections of the marketplace. The airport is a major Asian 'hub' operation, with 80 carriers flying to 180 cities in 50 countries and a passenger throughput of approximately 50 million. For many of these passengers it has become a 'destination hub', since those with an eight-hour wait for their onward flight are offered a choice of nearly 20 different styles of food, and if that is not enough there is even a rooftop garden and swimming pool available for their use. Hence all the awards. The airport is not resting on its laurels, for in 2008 a third terminal will open, increasing its capacity to 70 million.

Now the airport has taken luxury brands to a new and, for passengers, exciting level. Valiram Group, a well-known Asian franchisee of global luxury brands, has entered into an agreement with the airport authority, the Civil Aviation Authority of Singapore, and as a result the Valiram luxury brands retail site has been designed and built, the whole process taking only six months. Valiram are based in Kuala Lumpur, Malaysia and started their

airport travel retail business back in 1996 with a textile shop in Subang International Airport. The group has grown rapidly in recent years, as its Chief Operating Officer, Julian Levy, explains: 'We operate several stand-alone luxury airport bou-tiques both in Malaysia and Singapore including Hermès, Coach, Dunhill, Montblanc, Bally and Godiva, so this is a natural progression for us.'

The centre itself is freestanding and is situat-ed right in the centre near Passport Control. As a result of this strategic placement passengers cannot miss the island site. It is at the very heart of the passenger thoroughfare in Terminal 2 which serves the business community for long-haul flights.

Most major cities, especially the capital ones, have one road that is regarded by the fashion industry and clients alike as the luxury brand street. It has not come about by accident; get a few luxury brands together and the rest will fol-low. It makes common sense: the area becomes a one-stop shop as all the luxury brands are grouped together, making it an exclusive street that attracts the type of consumer who has the kind of disposable income necessary to frequent such shops. From the shopper's point of view it is easy to make price comparisons within a relatively small area; all the luxury brands have a perceived quality level which makes price one of the most

ABOVE The walk-through area showing the shop entrances of both Fendi and Hugo Boss together with the central area of 'product clusters' for luggage and bags.

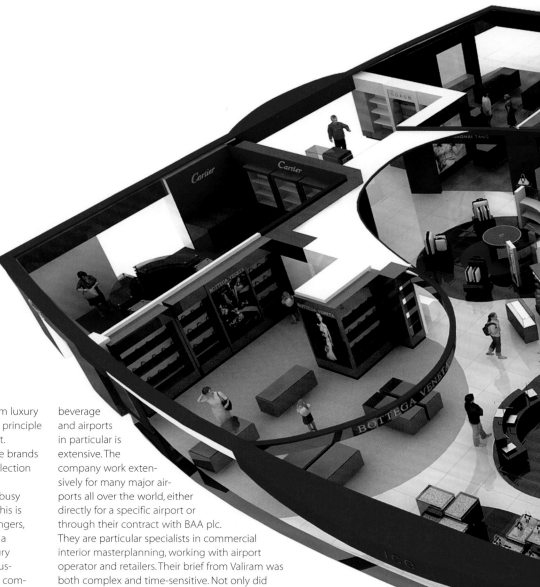

important choice mechanisms. The Valiram luxury brands centre works on exactly the same principle but here the space is even more compact.

How then does an airport put all these brands together – and what, if anything, is the selection procedure? Julian Levy explains:

In any major international airport the busy traveller is often limited for time and this is especially the case for business passengers, many of whom check in late. Being in a position to offer a broad range of luxury brands under one roof provides the customer with convenience, choice, price comparison which in turn enhances the shopping experience as well as sales. The brands that are on offer are selected based on their luxury, quality and sales potential. The brands featured are amongst the most prestigious and sought-after in the world and are high performers.

The Valiram concept is distinctively different from what happens in most airports around the world in that the company is a franchisee. It purchases the product range and then retails it through the luxury brands shops. The company has built up the ability to sell luxury brands to the Asian market over a number of years, and so was well placed to manage not only the luxury brand centre, but also the careful selection of what brands would be comparable and how the various different types of retailing methodology would work together in a confined space. This is where the meticulous design and masterplanning was to facilitate the Valiram dream.

The Valiram Group chose The Design Solution, whose depth of knowledge of retail, food and beverage and airports in particular is extensive. The company work extensively for many major airports all over the world, either directly for a specific airport or through their contract with BAA plc. They are particular specialists in commercial interior masterplanning, working with airport operator and retailers. Their brief from Valiram was both complex and time-sensitive. Not only did they have to design frontages according to the requirements of the brands themselves, but they also had to conceive a masterplan for the whole area so that the brands would be well balanced over the island site, allowing a free flow of passengers through it. The key item in all of this was the thoroughfare and the managing of it.

There were to be only three main entrances and on the 'back' walkway there was to be no entrance at all. This may seem rather restrictive at first glance but the five luxury brand shops on the back wall all have their own separate entrances on that perimeter, together with a second entrance/exit from or to the main body of the space. Another critical element to the design was to balance the individual shop frontage requirements, as all the shops are the same size. For both Bulgari and Cartier, situated on the two front corners, these were designed on the masterplan as stand-alone stores with no second entrance/exit into the main area. Flanking the main entrance are Fendi and Bottega Veneta, which are also both walk-through shops. The fluidity of footfall was

ABOVE This axonometric shows how the plan works in a more graphic way, complete with coloured walkways. It gives a clear and accurate bird's-eye view showing the five luxury brands across the back wall: Shanghai Tang, Chloé, Tod's, Salvatore Ferragamo and Hugo Boss. The two self-contained corner units are Cartier and Bulgari, with the entrance flanked by Bottega Veneta and Fendi. The central area is merchandised by product line rather than brand, and is bordered by Coach and Dunhill.

ABOVE The Swarovski luxury brand display is noticeably different from the other 'product cluster' branding.

critical for the project; it is exasperating for a shopper to retrace his or her steps in a shopping environment. It is counterproductive as it does not give the consumer something new to look at and experience, and it puts them in a negative frame of mind which does nothing to encourage purchases and so makes no commercial sense. The positioning of the most high-profile brands near to the relatively large main entrance also serves to draw customers in, benefiting some less prominent brands inside.

The 'interior' configuration works on the basis of a simple T-shape but has been designed in a more free-flowing, organic way, softening the structure and assisting a more even passenger flow. This is important when viewing the different retail scenario of the middle section for it is here that luxury brands operate on a 'product cluster' methodology. Separate sections for sunglasses and for luggage contain all the luxury brand names in each of those marketplaces. This variety of retailing is in no way secondary to the main luxury brand stores but further extends opportunities within the sector and assists passenger choice

and speed. A passenger simply would be unlikely to have the time or the inclination to visit 10 shops to select and try on sunglasses, but by putting all luxury brands for glasses together in one spot the traveller will instantly have more choice and is more likely to make a purchase.

The success of the site design and masterplan is also down to the difficult task of marrying up what the public perceive the brand to look like both externally and internally with what the airport will allow and need. Close co-operation between all parties is essential, for it is in everybody's best interests. This luxury brands marketplace is an expanding one; China was long regarded as a manufacturer of cheap goods for the world's various retail markets, but now has its own fast-expanding luxury brand in Shanghai Tang, and airports give the best brand exposure to the global customer. Luxury products are also high-profit items, so with growing global affluence companies such as Valiram will focus on this market more and more. Valiram have also submitted a bid for the new Changi Terminal 3 to operate a new luxury fashion concession there.

ABOVE Heavy luxury tax-free branding communicates to the passenger exactly what to expect in this retail area.

ABOVE RIGHT The brightly lit shops of both Fendi and Bulgari contrast with the more subdued illumination of the concourse.

BELOW The shop entrances of Shanghai Tang, Dior and Tod's off the central area.

A TRULY ENGLISH LUXURY BRAND

CASE STUDY: MULBERRY, HEATHROW AIRPORT, UK AND WORLDWIDE

**Designer: Four IV Design Consultants,
London, UK**

Mulberry is an English luxury lifestyle brand with a backbone of craftsmanship that has led to an extensive line of luxury bags designed for today's living. The business was started back in the 1970s by Roger Saul, located in a very rural Somerset which employed its own workforce from day one to design and exclusively craft the company's own products – not a common thing then, and even less so now. This was to be the basis on which Saul built the business into the brand it is today, although he is no longer part of the company, having become a hotelier.

The brand now has approaching 60 shops located in 17 countries around the world. It has doubled its size in the last five years and seen the percentage of its annual turnover that is from UK markets drop from 90 per cent to 70 per cent. This expansion is not just accounted for by the number of new stores opening, but also by moves to larger sites within the same area. It reflects the general business climate among luxury global brands as a whole.

Mulberry opened their first airport store 10 years ago in Heathrow's Terminal 4. They also had a franchise in Dubai. Five years ago they moved into Terminals 1 and 3, and they are soon to be in the new Terminal 5. There is also a Mulberry outlet at Stansted. All stores are located airside so as to

enjoy the tax-free sales break. The stores have not remained static; the earlier outlets were around 600 square feet in size, but now they operate out of 800 to 1200 square feet. Product density is very high due to the core nature of the Mulberry business. This pattern of corporate expansion is set to continue, with other airports already lined up in Scandinavia and the European Union.

As to why Mulberry moved into the airport luxury brand marketplace, it was the same motive as other brands: to enhance their international profile. Their first store at Heathrow Terminal 4 was specifically targeted at American passengers, which helped to give the brand a presence in that country without leaving England – and it is worth bearing in mind that the luxury brand market in the States is worth some 53 billion euros. Following the success of this American-targeted venture, the company expanded into other terminals to target the different global markets they serve.

The essence of the Mulberry brand and how it is portrayed to the global luxury community is of artisan-made, quality goods. The fact that the company crafts its own items is another point that reinforces the luxury element of the comprehensive range of products. If it so chose, the company could further reinforce the luxury brand message

ABOVE Mulberry, Heathrow Terminal 3. The high illumination of the luggage and handbag display units contrasts with the almost whimsical product display of the adjacent slat wall.

by publicising its activities in relation to starting apprenticeship schemes to enable Mulberry to nurture and develop young craftspeople, not to mention to fuel the continual and rising demand. From their own brand perspective this is their greatest challenge.

Another of the brand messages is concerned with tactility – encouraging passengers to become involved in the product, to have a relationship. This is all further assisted by the fact that it is English: English design, not just a UK-based company. The brand messages are all targeted at the departing passenger but this message also works back home in that its success has been to draw shoppers into its UK stores. Presumably this works equally well in its outlets around the world.

Building all these luxury brand messages into a store's design seems a tricky business, but Mulberry have used the same company that created their

flagship store in Bond Street, London back in 2001. The London-based company, Four IV Design Consultants, had taken what was previously a rather dowdy corporate design and given it a much more upmarket look – in their own words 'created a contemporary metro design nous cut with Britishness'. Four IV are well known in the luxury brand market for their work with brands such as Wedgwood, Thomas Pink, and major stores like Harrods, Liberty and Harvey Nichols. One of the main strengths to this consultancy is that it offers a fully integrated design service, managing not only the shop design and layout but also the corporate identity graphics that are so important to luxury brand retailers.

Over the last 10 years the concept has changed remarkably little, but what has changed a lot is the footfall. How this is planned into the Mulberry terminal shop is critical. This too goes

 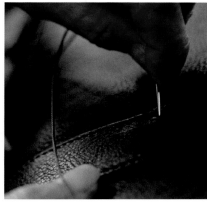 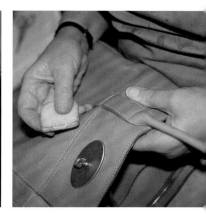

ABOVE LEFT TO RIGHT
Where the whole creative process starts, at the raw materials store.

Luxury at its best: the final touches of hand-stitching to a Mulberry handbag.

Perfecting the final product by rubbing off the block marks by hand.

BELOW A luxury brand is born: the Mulberry tree.

hand-in-hand with how the products are displayed – some under glass for security, and others so that the passenger can fully interact with them. While staffing costs are similar to the company's non-airport outlets, the expense of design and fit-out is 15–20 per cent higher per square metre. Mulberry, like most operators in an airport, know that the passenger audience can change from day to day and in some cases from hour to hour, depending on flight arrivals and destinations, so there is a greater emphasis on display and presentation of product. Their shop in Heathrow's

Terminal 3 relies heavily on a sophisticated graphic language to attract, almost like a billboard. The enormous shop window thus provides a good opportunity to reinforce the luxury brand message.

Each of the stores, although fully representing the Mulberry brand ethos, is designed on a bespoke basis and personalised in product range according to where it is situated. All stores work on a very high density of product, and according to the company all trade at the same levels despite having different international passengers passing through the different terminals. The product range

ABOVE Mulberry, Heathrow Terminal 3. Here the luxury brand's corporate colour is used to good effect on both floor and cabinets.

RIGHT Mulberry, Heathrow Terminal 3. The shop interior created by Four IV Design produces a calm effect and makes the product look special.

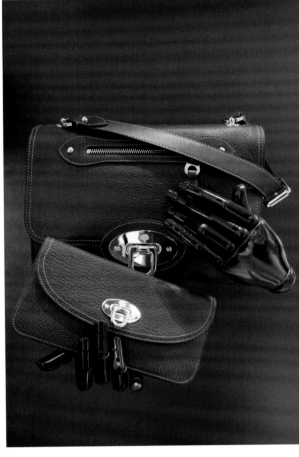

is critical so, for instance, there are no fashion ranges sold in any of the airport outlets. Their luggage range is one of their best sellers and one in which they are internationally known. This particular product grouping must be attractive both in quality and tax break because anybody travelling through an airport already has luggage with them. With the increased security measures adopted at all international airports, carry-on luggage and bags have assumed a greater importance, so if your bag conforms to the maximum permitted size and is a luxury brand it is a win-win situation. As a consequence sales for Mulberry in this type and variety of luggage have grown considerably.

The company has also developed another selling method at airports called Mulberry Touch

Point, a small online unit where items can be ordered, paid for and delivered to an address of your choice without the complications of carriage. It still carries the same tax break. Each unit will be linked to the nearest high-street store and managed by them. When Terminal 5 finally opens at London's Heathrow, Mulberry are going to offer an 'at gate' or 'at lounge' delivery service, which is another way of reinforcing a luxury brand image.

Luxury brands such as Mulberry must leave no stone unturned in their quest to be different. If the products are 'luxury' then services such as Mulberry's could well prove the deciding factor for customers considering whether to make a purchase, or which luxury brand to choose.

LEFT Mulberry, Heathrow Terminal 3. The product as an icon. Here each larger luxury item is displayed surrounded by ample space, and small items are presented in a secure but not imposing wooden merchandising cabinet.

TOP LEFT Mulberry, centre of Paris store. An overall view of just how Mulberry displays its luxury bag range on a plain wall.

TOP RIGHT Mulberry, centre of Paris store. Sophisticated product display and merchandising combined.

A CHINESE LUXURY BRAND

CASE STUDY: SHANGHAI TANG, HONG KONG INTERNATIONAL AIRPORT

During the 1920s and 1930s, Shanghai was often called 'the Paris of the East'. It did have that touch of decadence that so befitted those times, evident throughout the world. Glamour and luxury were omnipresent, with the likes of Charlie Chaplin, George Bernard Shaw, Noël Coward and Aldous Huxley making it a 'must-go' place. It was a melting pot of people and styles.

Shanghai Tang was founded back in 1994 by Hong Kong businessman David Tang Wing-Cheung. The name Shanghai Tang evokes the elegance of a time gone by in Shanghai, but this first 'luxury' Chinese brand has now put the city back on the world map. In its first year the store attracted over one million visitors, and by the year 2000 footfall had passed four million. The business is a mixture of retail offer encompassing women's, men's and children's attire, accessories, homewares and gifts. This would be an impressive offer for any new brand; for a luxury one it is almost unheard-of in such a short space of time. As part of its Chinese luxury brand 'story' it also has Imperial Tailors, a sub-brand which has revived the diminishing art of Chinese *haute-couture* culture using all the magical colours and materials found back in the 1920s and 1930s. The brand identity is based on Chinese designs and culture combined with the dynamism of the 21st century. To call it a bold step

would be patronising; it is an understanding that the luxurious lifestyles of yesteryear can be brought back, contemporised and shown as a confident luxury retail offer for the modern world to enjoy.

The opening up of China and the change in political status of Hong Kong has led to more international passenger traffic, mainly into China as Western businesspeople seek new opportunities and develop more business links. It does not necessarily follow that luxury brands spring up as affluence grows; they take both time to nurture and a great deal of targeted marketing, in which the founder David Tang has been particularly successful.

Shanghai Tang's entrée into the dynamic world of airport luxury retailing was in 1998, only five years after its own first store opening. This brave step was on home soil at Hong Kong International Airport in a building known as Chep Lap Kok which was one of the most expensive airports ever built, costing $19.9 billion. Its passenger terminal is the largest enclosed space in the world and services over 600 aircraft and 113,000 passengers per day.

Shanghai Tang's first luxury store opened in a 33-square-metre space situated in the Terminal Atrium at the East Hall of the airport. This position proved most popular for last-minute passenger

ABOVE The store has an almost zigzag configuration.
Effective use of the bright corporate colours draws people into a potentially awkward-shaped shop.

LEFT Shanghai Tang, Ngee Ann City, Singapore. This city store displays key internal details that have also been used in Shanghai Tang's airport stores. The carpet is one of the less obvious elements that make up the design jigsaw.

BELOW The store interior demonstrates the very effective use of the essential Chinese corporate colours combined with the dark wood merchandising units.

ABOVE Although this is a city store, the graphics and wood are part of the same design family used at the brand's airport outlets. Even product display and illumination are the same.

OVERLEAF The product range in all its colourful glory. Here all the items are simply displayed against a coloured backdrop together with dark wood.

shopping. More importantly, it exposed the still young luxury brand to a very large world market. The original store was a concession but, with the rapid global expansion of the brand, Shanghai Tang bought their partner out in 2004 and developed the store even further, opening another store within Chep Lap Kok.

This showcase of Chinese luxury was pivotal in the company's expansion plans. It now has 22 stores around the world specifically located in luxury hotspots. There are no prizes for guessing where they are: London, Paris, New York, Zurich, Tokyo, Bangkok, Honolulu, to name but a few. More are to follow – Las Vegas, Macau and Kuala Lumpur are all on the Shanghai Tang list of preferred locations. Five of the 22 boutiques are airport sites. Here it becomes clear just how important airport retail is for a luxury brand, as in Taiwan their only store is in Taiwan Taoyuan International Airport. It is the exposure to a constant stream of affluent people of the world, who not only purchase a product or two but also buy into the brand as a

luxury purchase, that is so important in spreading the brand message.

Why has Shanghai Tang been so successful? It is easy enough to market yourself as China's first luxury brand – but convincing an extremely sophisticated global consumer market that you are, and that you have something different to offer them, is a totally different matter. So, what does Shanghai Tang stand for and why? Corine Pin, Strategic Marketing Manager of Shanghai Tang, explains:

The company is a lifestyle vision of Chinese-inspired chic with a modern sensibility. Shanghai Tang is currently the only luxury brand emerging from China and we see ourselves as an aesthetic ambassador of the fastest-growing nation in the world. We aim at producing the best from Chinese culture, synthesised with contemporary elements and trends to create wearable, relevant, commercial products, to be a globally compelling brand, appealing to sophisticated

ABOVE The lighting, subdued in parts, highlights
the clothes and products on display.

affluent consumers. Finally we pride ourselves for being the first Chinese lifestyle brand going west.

Shanghai Tang themselves have designed and developed the store concept of 'East meets West' over all their airport outlets, and it is given a bespoke treatment at each of the boutiques dependent on location and store size. These two critical elements, location and size, also play a significant part in the company's product selection procedure. Like most of the luxury brand interior designs, Shanghai Tang's own team developed what they now have in-store by taking the most appropriate elements and utilising them in the airport situation. What the company has done is to develop the concept into identifying the most important design and visual elements, and then to structure each boutique's design around these prominent features, so that the very best of the luxury brand concept will shine through. This is particularly vital where the stores are small. Part of the brand story is Shanghai Tang's in-store presentation, enabling customers to choose from a wide product universe. The result is that each boutique has its own characteristics but still fits into the concept of 'East meets West'.

The benefit of airport retail, probably more to luxury brands than to others, is that it provides an opportunity for passengers who may not otherwise have shopped during their trip to do so. For Shanghai Tang, product selection is both complex and critical – complex because their normal full range of merchandise is so extensive, and critical due to the perennial airport problem of limited space. What the company has set out to do, and has done very successfully, is to offer the passenger a carefully chosen selection from all their separate markets. The selection process is also based on the simple fact that people are travelling, so the offer is very much adapted to their needs and comprises a larger selection of smaller and easy-to-carry luxury goods. With European trade especially buoyant, this method works extremely well – Europe is a tough market to break into as it already has most of the world's luxury brands within its own geographical area.

Airports are a key element in Shanghai Tang's future expansion plans and they are taking it even further by opening up airline in-flight shops with Cathay Pacific and JAL. The success is phenomenal and will obviously inspire other Chinese entrepreneurs to follow. All of this has been accomplished in a remarkably short time and airports have been at the forefront of developing this particular luxury brand message.

SECURING LUXURY

CASE STUDIES: SWAROVSKI, FILA AND MULBERRY DISPLAY UNITS

Designers: Carter Design Group and Four IV Design Consultants

Luxury brand items are important. They are also treasured by their owners for many reasons – some practical, others aesthetic. As a consequence, there is a huge counterfeit market in luxury brand goods. Watches, bags and perfume, to name just three, are all copied in multi-million-dollar brand theft. There is also the more obvious form of theft – that of taking the genuine products and not paying for them.

Companies such as Mulberry, along with other brands that market small luxury items in an airport terminal, have a persistent problem despite an element of critical design that will control such activity. Mulberry's Chief Operating Officer Lisa Montague commented: 'As a brand we talk about artisan qualities, touch, and tactile feel so it is important that customers can do this. For the larger luggage products security is not so bad but for the smaller items we have to secure the display as much as possible without offending.' Small items can be on public view but under glass; merchandising units can be specially designed to allow maximum product display to potential customers but with security built in that does not offend the potential purchaser.

Carter Design Group, based in Leicestershire, have a long history of designing units for jewellery, watches and accessories for major luxury brands. The company's Chairman, John Carter, explains:

Over a long time now we have been asked by several luxury brand companies to design display cabinets and merchandising units that had an element of security built into them. We have achieved this not by using locks and bars that people can see and that would therefore put them off, but by simple slide-release mechanisms to enable the assistants to easily demonstrate and show whatever item the customer wanted to see. These units can come in any shape or size and are designed and made to the luxury brand owner's specification. We have found that our approach to design, with security being just a part rather than being the overriding factor, works very well for brands that want the products to be on display and able to be touched by customers. It is very much to everyone's liking, and promotes sales.

For major luxury brands, staff training in security is now *de rigueur* and part of selling procedure at airports where theft takes place. One of the disadvantages of airport terminal store design in comparison to the high-street counterpart is that there is no 'front door' – in fact for many retail outlets in airports there are no physical barriers at all, making theft that much easier. Steve Collis, Managing Director of JHP Design, gives some

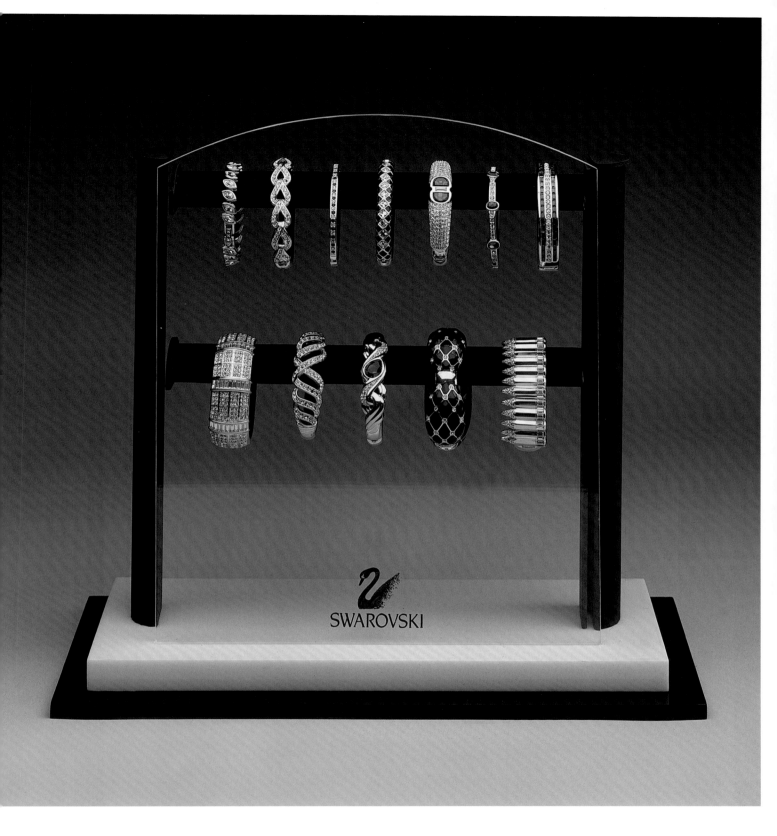

ABOVE Swarovski display unit. Here all the bangles and bracelets can not only be seen but also touched, an important quality for luxury brand merchandise. The only time an item will be removed is for personal fitting. The elegance of the design, by Carter Design Group, enables the product, rather than the unit, to be king.

TOP LEFT Mulberry display unit. A very secure unit displays the belts as they would be worn, with the buckle foremost. It allows the customer to touch and feel the tactile qualities of the leather. The leather display adds an air of quality to the product range, thereby making the selection process that bit more enjoyable.

TOP RIGHT Mulberry display unit. The specially designed merchandising unit shows how, even when the drawers are open, the small items are still displayed in a beautiful manner. It also does not offend the customer; in fact it could be viewed as an Aladdin's cave of products.

useful tips on the differences between airport and high-street store layouts:

Airport shops are different for many practical things, not just security. There are few shop fronts, as we know, and any units will have ample space around them for ease of customer flow. Product security is about keeping small high-priced items that all luxury brands sell at airports under glass but – and this is important – with well-trained staff, so that the personal service element of bringing an item out for the customer to look at more closely is seen by that person as a benefit rather than a barrier. The natural open spaces of airport retail actually help keep the products secure because there are less hidden or dark areas. This is about as much as you can hope for apart from natural staff diligence.

Luxury brand theft does happen at airports, so

what are the contingencies and safeguards? This differs from airport operator to airport operator and even airline to airline. If a luxury brand item is stolen, the chances are that it is airside so there are no passport or security barriers to pass through. A tracking procedure can be put into operation where a theft is known, and if necessary a passenger will be taken from the aircraft that he or she has boarded, for on an aircraft it is not possible to get rid of an item as easily as in a terminal. The consequences for that passenger are dire, for not only do they face prosecution but also they miss their flight and therefore have to re-book, a costly procedure all round.

Design and staff training are two essential tools for luxury brand companies. Mulberry, because of the type of products sold, have developed a very proactive relationship between these two elements, to lessen the possibility of theft.

RIGHT Fila display unit. On the left-hand side of the unit there is a simple white strip of plastic which acts as a release mechanism for the unit's door. Created by Carter Design Group, it is unobtrusive and easy to operate.

BELOW Mulberry display unit. This unit constructed of both glass and wood displays the wide variety of leather wallets, enabling customers to select the items they want prior to requesting service.

LISTING

ARCHITECTS AND DESIGNERS

Architectural Alliance
400 Clifton Avenue South
Minneapolis
Minnesota 55403
USA
+1 612 871 5703

Arup
13 Fitzroy Street
London W1T 4BQ
England
+44 (0)207 636 1531

Barber Design Consultants
Studio 17
The Royal Victoria Patriotic Building
Trinity Road
London SW18 3SX
England
+44 (0)208 870 5335

Carter Design Group
North Lane
Foxton
Market Harborough
Leicestershire LE16 7RF
England
+44 (0)1858 433 322
www.carterdesign.co.uk

Cesar Pelli & Associates/Pelli Clarke Pelli Architects
1056 Chapel Street
New Haven
Connecticut 06510
USA
+1 203 777 2515

Douglas Wallace
1 Grantham Street
Dublin 8
Ireland
+353 1 478 7500

Estudio Lamela
Calle O'Donnell 34
6th Floor
28009 Madrid
Spain
+34 91 574 3600

Fitch
121–141 Westbourne Terrace
London W2 6JR
England
+44 (0)207 479 0900

Four IV
4th Floor
11 Northburgh Street
London EC1V 0AN
England
+ 44 (0)207 336 1344
www.fouriv.com

HOK Aviation
620 Avenue of the Americas
New York
New York 10011
USA
+1 212 741 1200

JHP Design
Unit 2
6 Erskine Road
London NW3 3AJ
England
+44 (0)207 722 3932

K+P Architects
Ismaninger Strasse 57
D-81675 München
Germany
+49 89 41 1188-0

Kohn Pedersen Fox Architects
111 West 57th Street
New York
New York 10019
USA
+1 212 977 6500

Murphy/Jahn
35 East Wacker Drive
Chicago
Illinois 60601
USA
+1 312 427 7300

Rogers Stirk Harbour + Partners
Thames Wharf
Rainville Road
London W6 9HA
England
+44 (0)207 385 1235

Softroom
341 Oxford Street
London WC1 2JE
England
+44 (0)207 408 0864

Sunderland Innerspace Design
Suite 400
1788 West 5th Avenue
Vancouver V6J 1P2
Canada
+1 604 662 7015

Studio Architetto Mar
Via Castellana 60
30174 Venezia Zelarino
Italy
+39 041 984 477

Studio Linse
Keizersgracht 534
1017 EK Amsterdam
The Netherlands
+31 (0)20 675 4798

The Design Solution
90 Westbourne Grove
London W2 5RT
England
+44 (0)207 556 5300

Woodhead International
26-28 Chesser Street
Adelaide
Australia 5000
+61 (8) 8223 5013

LEFT The Charles de Gaulle airport, Paris.
Terminal 2 at night showing the stunning
Hotel Sheraton in the centre.

Listing   229

AIRPORT PLANNERS AND ENGINEERS

Bechtel
11 Pilgrim Street
London EC4 6RN
England
+44 (0)207 651 7777
www.bechtel.com

Baxall Ltd
Unit 1, Castlehill
Horsfield Way
Bredbury Park Industrial Estate
Stockport SK6 2SU
England
+44 (0)161 406 6611
www.baxall.com

Airworthiness Worldwide
1820 Long Creek Court
Granbury
Texas 76049
USA
+1 817 573 0220
www.airworthinessworldwide.com

DSSR
Craven House
40 Uxbridge Road
Ealing
London W5 2TZ
England
+44 (0)208 567 5621
www.dssr.co.uk

IPM Ltd
Room 141, 1st Floor, Longbridge House
North Terminal
Gatwick Airport
West Sussex RH6 0PJ
England
+44 (0)1293 504468
www.ipm-ltd.co.uk

URS Corporation
600 Montgomery Street 26th Floor
San Francisco, CA 94111-2728
USA
+1 415 774 2700
www.urscorp.com

W&P
Uhlemeyerstrasse 9+11
D-30175 Hannover
Germany
+49 511 34 1414
www.wp-architects.com

AIRPORT FIT-OUT AND INTERIOR STRUCTURE COMPANIES

Aigis Blast Protection Ltd
Sinfin Central Business Park
Sinfin Lane
Derby DE24 9GL
England
+44 1332 273577
www.aegis.co.uk

Decoustics Ltd
65 Disco Road
Toronto
Ontario M9W 1M2
Canada
+1 416 675 3983
www.decoustics.com

Figueras International Seating
08186 Lliçà d'Amunt
Barcelona
Spain
+34 93 844 5060
www.figueras.com

GKD
Gebr Kufferath AG
Metallweberstrasse 46
D-52353 Düren
Germany
+49 24 21 8030
www.creativeweave.de

IMAT
Paduleta, 3 – (P.I. Jundiz)
P.O. Box 5032 AP
01015 Vitoria
Spain
+34 945 220 048
www.imat.es

Lindner Airports Worldwide
Bahnhofstrasse 29
94424 Arnstorf
Germany
+49 87 2320 2534
www.lindner-airports.com

Rimex Metals Ltd
Aden Road
Ponders End
Enfield
Middlesex EN3 7SU
England
+44 (0)208 804 0633
www.rimexmetals.com

Trespa International BV
Wetering 20
PO Box 110
6000 AC Weert
The Netherlands
+31 495 458 356
www.trespa.com

LIGHTING COMPANIES

Lighting Design House
The Studio
380 Great West Road
Hounslow
Middlesex TW5 0PB
England
+44 (0)208 572 3852
www.lightingdesignhouse.com

Speirs and Major Associates
Well Court Hall
Dean Village
Edinburgh EH4 3BE,
Scotland
+44 (0)131 226 4474
www.samassociates.com

Thorn Lighting Ltd
Silver Screens
Elstree Way
Borehamwood
Hertfordshire WD6 1FE
England
+44 (0)208 732 9800
www.thornlighting.com

BAGGAGE HANDLING

Inter-Roller Engineering Ltd
20 Benoi Crescent
Singapore
+65 6861 2828
www.inter-roller.com

Lyngsoe Systems
Lyngsø Allé 3
DK-9600 Aars
Denmark
+45 96 980 980
www.lyngsoesystems.com

AIRPORT SEATING

Airport Seating Alliance
813 Ridge Lake Boulevard
Suite 401
Memphis
TN 38120
USA
+1 901 685 8263
www.airportseatingalliance.com

Arconas
580 Orwell Street
Mississauga
Ontario L5A 3V7
Canada
+1 905 272 0727
www.arconas.com

ENEA
Ola Auzoa 4
20250 Legorreta
Guipúzcoa
Spain
+34 943 806275
www.eneacontract.com

Ferfor
Calle La Guardiola 1
08793 Avinyonet del Penedès
Barcelona
Spain
+34 93 897 0029
www.ferfor.com

OMK Design
Stephen Building
30 Stephen Street
London W1T 1QR
England
+44 (0)207 631 1335
www.omkdesign.com

AIRPORT COMMUNICATIONS

Aviavox
Star Parc
Boeing Avenue 271
1119 PD Schiphol-Rijk
The Netherlands
+31 (0)20 750 6760
www.aviavox.com

CONRAC
Lindenstrasse 8
D-97990 Weikersheim
Germany
+49 7934 1010
www.conrac.de

Vogel's Products BV
Hondsruglaan 93
5628 DB Eindhoven
The Netherlands
+31 (0)40 264 7400
www.vogels.com

AIRPORT ORGANISATIONS

British Airport Services & Equipment Association
Homelife House
26–32 Oxford Road
Bournemouth BH8 8EZ
England
+44 (0)1202 299 088
www.basea.org.uk

IATA
800 Place Victoria
Box 113
Montreal, Quebec H4Z 1M1
Canada
+1 514 874 0202
www.iata.org

AIRPORT PUBLICATIONS

Aéroportuaire Magazine
18 Avenue Parmentier
75011 Paris
France
+33 1 4730 1950

Airports International
1–4 Gwash Way
Stamford
Lincolnshire PE9 1XQ
England
+44 (0)1780 755131
www.airportsint.com

Buying Business Travel
2nd Floor, Cardinal House
39–40 Albemarle Street
London W1S 4TE
England
+44 (0)207 647 6363
www.buyingbusinesstravel.com

Jane's Airport Review
1 Sentinel House
163 Brighton Road
Coulsdon
Surrey CR5 2YH
England
+44 (0)208 700 3700
www.Jar@janes.com

Passenger Terminal World
Abinger House
Church Street
Dorking
Surrey RH4 1DF
England
+44 (0)1306 743 744

Wanderlust
PO Box 1832
Windsor
Berkshire SL4 1YT
England
+44 (0)1753 620 426
www.wanderlust.co.uk

Listing   231

SELECT BIBLIOGRAPHY

Robert Horonjeff and Francis McKelvey, *Planning & Design of Airports* (McGraw Hill, New York, 1993)

Hugh Pearman, *Airports: A Century of Architecture* (Abrams, New York, 2004)

Antonin Kazda and Robert Caves, *Airport Design and Operation* (Pergamon, London, 2000)

Richard de Neufville & Amedeo Odoni, *Airport Systems: Planning, Design and Management* (McGraw Hill, New York, 2002)

Archibald Black, *American Airport Designs, containing 44 prize winning and other drawings from the Lehigh Airports Competition* (Taylor, Rogers and Bliss, New York, 1930)